Ship To:

AP-TP - 1033648-1-0210
Main Address
800 Avondale Ave
1033648-1-0210
Grandview Heights, OH 43212

AF535162

Buyer PO #: 1033648-1-0210

Order ID: 113-1426323-4645030

Thank you for buying from Danbury Railway Museum on Amazon Marketplace.

Shipping Address:	Order Date:	Wed, Jul 8, 2026
AP-TP	Shipping Service:	Standard
Main Address	Buyer Name:	CollegeBooksDirect
800 Avondale Ave	Seller Name:	Danbury Railway Museum
1033648-1-0210		
Grandview Heights, OH		
43212		

Quantity	Product Details
1	**Texas Electric album, Texas Electric Railway (Interurbans special) [Paperback] [1975] Varney, Rod** **SKU:** BF-W1GT-RE1B **ASIN:** 0916374017 **Condition:** Used - Acceptable **Order Item ID:** 164342143357721 **Condition note:** A slightly bumped corner and some other minor wear. Proceeds benefit the Danbury Railway Museum Collection Fund.

Returning your item:

Go to "Your Account" on Amazon.com, click "Your Orders" and then click the "seller profile" link for this order to get information about the return and refund policies that apply.

Visit https://www.amazon.com/returns to print a return shipping label. Please have your order ID ready.

Thanks for buying on Amazon Marketplace. To provide feedback for the seller please visit www.amazon.com/feedback. To contact the seller, go to Your Orders in Your Account. Click the seller's name under the appropriate product. Then, in the "Further Information" section, click "Contact the Seller."

Texas Electric Album

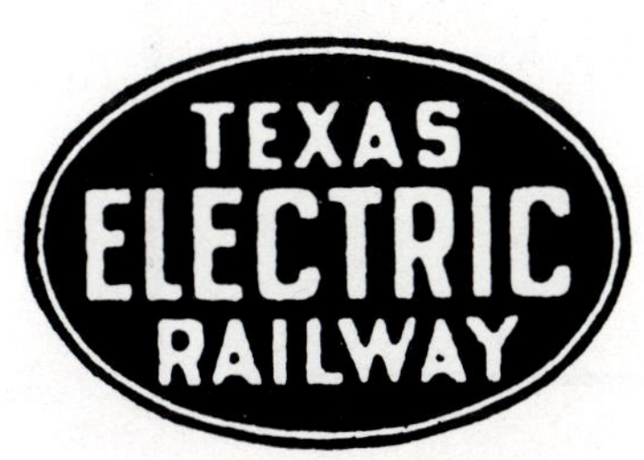

Rod Varney and the Texas ERA

INTERURBANS SPECIAL 62

Interurbans

Estate of Ira L. Swett, Harry W. Swett, Executor. Executor's address: PO Box 201, Claremont, California 91711.

Permanent Interurbans Address (Correspondence only): PO Box 6444 Glendale, California 91205

Publisher . . . . **Mac Sebree**
Editor . . . . **Jim Walker**

Texas Electric Album

By Rod Varney and the Texas ERA

Interurbans Special 62

Southern Traction 8

Price: $6.50

First Printing: Autumn 1975
ISBN 0-916 374-01-7
Printed in the United States of America

Photo Credits:

I: Interurbans Archives
MC: Magna Collection
MS: Collection of Mac Sebree
TERA: Texas ERA Collection
(Other photos credited individually)

Cover Photo:

DEEP IN THE HEART OF TEXAS, there existed during the second, third, fourth and fifth decades of this century a remarkably fine interurban system, with some of the handsomest cars ever to operate in the U.S. Here comes one of them, the "Blue Bonnet," rolling down the famed Trinity River Viaduct towards its Dallas terminal. The date is April 10, 1940; the photographer is Charles D. Savage—and the railroad is the Texas Electric. No. 310 is running as train No. 628, left Corsicana at 3:40PM, and is about to tie up at the Dallas Interurban Terminal at 5:30PM. The "Blue Bonnet" was the pride of the system—a named train with spit 'n polish equipment and on-time performance expected. When you add classic arch-windowed equipment like this, who could ask for more?

Map on inside covers
Walter P. Donalson, Jr.

☆ Foreword

THE INSPIRATION for this Texas Electric Album came from Neill Boldrick, Jr., of San Antonio who wanted every traction fan to share his enthusiasm for this great interurban. Boldrick, a long-time member of the Texas Division, Electric Railroaders' Association, took the idea to Rod Varney and TERA directors who quickly caught Boldrick's enthusiasm for this project and accepted his challenge.

This is not by any means a history of the Texas Electric. Boldrick specified that it not delve into the details of the line's construction, operation, rolling stock, or specifics of any kind. Rather, it is a photo album illustrating some mighty fine country and some of the handsomest interurban equipment which ever rolled. We have attempted to capture the unique flavor of the Texas Electric and to portray the rich diversity of its operations. The full story, however, awaits the reader in another book, by veteran Texas traction historian Johnnie Myers to be issued as a forthcoming Central Electric Railfans Association yearbook.

The Boldrick Foundation provided the seed money to get things underway. To Rod Varney, founder and chief exhorter of the Texas ERA (and mulepower proponent extraordinaire) fell the job of assembling the large amount of photographic material loaned to the division for this task. And what a rich lode of photos it was—many of the most stalwart chroniclers of the Texas Electric contributed including Charles D. Savage, M.D. McCarter and Walter P. Donalson. Others, including Charles A. Smallwood and C.V. Hess, opened up their extensive collections. What you see in this volume represents the pick of many hundreds of fine photos.

Ol' Rod wrote the captions, instilling in the continuity his unique flavor for telling a story accurately but entertainingly—you can almost hear the drawl. Originally the plan was for the Texas ERA to publish this album independently as Southern Traction #8, but it soon became apparent that in order to do justice to the topic it would be necessary to enlist the cooperation of a professional traction publisher. *Interurbans* thus became a willing and enthusiastic partner in the enterprise, for the Texas Electric had always been a favorite of both late publisher Ira L. Swett and his successor, and the Magna Collection and the *Interurbans* Archives provided some additional material. As a matter of fact, this book marks *Interurbans'* second visit to the Lone Star State; **Interurbans Special 22,** by Herb Woods, provided the story of the Galveston-Houston Electric Railway back in 1959.

Today there is little to remind the visitor to Northern Texas' rolling green fields of the passing of the cream and crimson electrics, save for an occasional culvert, bridge abutment or raised earth grade. This volume will, we hope, rekindle in some small measure the spirit of this fine interurban for those fortunate enough to have ridden it, and to serve as an introduction to traction at its finest to those who never had the chance.

Autumn, 1975 MAC SEBREE

Introduction to the Texas Division, ERA and Membership Information

The members of the Texas Division, Electric Railroaders' Association, are held together by the common bond of publications and most important of all, just plain writing letters to each other. There are no meetings to attend. Your letters and our Board of Directors do everything needed to keep us going.

Three publications come your way. One, and the most important, is the monthly Short Circuit Bulletin (SCB). The 10th of the month is when anything that the members have sent in is poured into the SCB and mailed out shortly thereafter. Only what YOU as members send in gets into the SCB. Your Editor doesn't put in anything except his sassy remarks. Letters are the main ingredient of each issue.

The second publication is the so-called "southern traction annals." (Note the lower case letters.) It is an "if and when" bulletin issued when subject matter comes along that is too long for SCB. The third publication comes more infrequently and is called "Southern Traction" (ST), and usually contains a complete history of one system and is published in book or booklet form. This Interurbans Special 62 is an expanded version of Southern Traction.

About back issues: with SCB you can get any year, 1963 through 1974, for $3.00 per year. sta and ST are also available. (sta's are, for the most part, out of print, but Xerox copies will be made at cost.)

Goodies! This is the Texas Division Extra! With each SCB comes a supply of things the members send you as a gift. We're talking about such things as post cards, timetables, maps, advertising literature, feature letters from contributors such as Luis Leon T., George Horn, Dick Bowker, Ralph Forty, Tom Williams, David Sickles, Steve Scalzo, Ray De Groote, Warwick Jenkins, Bill Bolton, Jack O'Meara, Joe Canfield, Bobby Peschkes. All are free! Your $4.00 annual dues doesn't cover the cost of all this; in many cases the authors themselves print and send in their letters. Some send a contribution to cover the printing.

Let's go back to your membership. It is by invitation only. We do not seek volume but rather dedication to our main interest, traction history. Most of the members are either authors, serious researchers, or are so doggone nuts about traction that we can't keep them away. You can recommend a friend but don't send his application unless he is at least half nuts. Your $4.00 covers the monthly SCB only; everything else must be donated (deductible), sta's, ST's and Goodies. Extra donations are usually needed—and always appreciated.

ROD VARNEY

☆ The Texas Electric

THE BIG, bright, bountiful state of Texas has always been a land of superlatives. Largest state in the union (until Alaska was admitted not so long ago), it had the biggest skies, the brightest stars, the most oil, the finest cattle, the prettiest girls and the ruggedest cowboys. All this made Texans inclined to boast a bit, secure in the belief that they had the best of everything.

Surprising it is, then, that among railfans Texas in general, and Dallas in particular, did not always get the credit for having one of the finest interurban systems in the country. For indeed it did. The Texas Electric Railway was a system of some 250 miles in length, ranking it with some of the premier lines of Ohio and Indiana, and exceeding any of the major systems radiating from Chicago. The Texas Electric operated some of the handsomest cars in the land, yet photographs of them do not begin to match in volume the illustrative heritage of a North Shore or an Indiana Railroad. The Texas Electric made Dallas into one of the busiest interurban centers in the nation; its seven-track downtown Interurban Terminal bustled day and night with the arrivals and departures of the cream and crimson interurbans to Waco, to Denison, to Corsicana and other north Texas centers of urban import. Two other companies sent cars out of Big D in three other directions; included was the Northern Texas Traction link to Dallas' sister city, Fort Worth —a busy line indeed for many years.

The Texas Electric was a true railroad in all senses of the word. It had all the sights, sounds and smells of the traditional line-haul railroad with the added attraction of electricity. Built rather late in the interurban construction era, the TE endeavored to be a model of modernity in the realm of intercity transport. In the 'teens and twenties, it **was** the last word in intercity travel.

In the early days of this century, the steam railroads were unwilling or unable to offer the kind of frequent local passenger service demanded by the growing economy, and the automobile was still a rich man's toy. Into this void stepped the new electric railway technology. Interurban railways, at first merely rural extensions of city streetcar lines, stretched out to link important urban centers offering fast, frequent and cheap passenger service. When the Texas Electric came into existence, the Lone Star State already had an electric interurban successfully operating the 10 miles between Denison and Sherman. The Denison & Sherman Railway Co. was the state's pioneer line, opened in 1901. A year later Dallas and Fort Worth were linked by interurban and this new form of transport was entrenched.

Into this picture stepped Col. J.F. Strickland, a Texas entrepreneur who formed the Texas Traction Co. to build a 67-mile interurban between Dallas and Sherman. It opened for business on July 1, 1908. Strickland had already purchased a substantial part of the stock of the D&S Co., so the next step was to combine the two end-to-end properties. This was done by April of 1911, when cars began making the through run between Dallas and Denison. Now the Texas Traction Co. had 77 miles of main line with local streetcar operations in Denison, Sherman and McKinney and with the repair shops at Denison.

This was a time of high optimism in Texas, as to the future of the Lone Star State and its economy, and to the future of electric railways as well. The management firm of Stone & Webster, operators of the Dallas street railway system and the Fort Worth-Dallas interurban, were now eyeing the possibilities south of Dallas. Corsicana was enjoying one of the state's early oil booms, while Waco reigned supreme as King Cotton's hometown. Things looked ripe for Stone & Webster penetration of these prime transportation markets.

The Strickland interests turned their attention southward at the same time. At first working independently, the two companies quickly decided to join forces to open up the southern territory and at this time the S&W-projected Dallas Southern Traction Co. was reorganized in 1912 to become the Southern Traction Co., reflecting the alliance with the Strickland forces, the latter taking over active management of the property.

The public was invited to invest in the new enterprise, and construction of both southern lines began simultaneously. The 97-mile main line to Waco was opened on October 12, 1913, and eight days later a shiny new interurban car rumbled the 53.7 miles into Corsicana for the first time. The shops for the new company were built at a location four miles south of Dallas where the line to Corsicana diverged. Completed in 1914, these facilities were given the name of Monroe Shops and also served as office headquarters until administrative functions were transferred to the new $1.5 million Dallas Interurban Building in mid-1916.

The next—and logical—step was to merge the two properties into one company, and on January 1, 1917, the Texas Electric Railway came into being. The stockholders of Texas Traction and Southern Traction agreed to swap stock creating a new interurban system of approximately 250 miles in length—longest in the entire South. With this expansion the company also acquired additional local lines in Waxahachie and Waco.

In its day, the TE was considered highly aggressive. First and second-class express service was instituted, offering a really fast and inexpensive package delivery system which was greatly appreciated by the many wholesale houses in Dallas. Railway Post Office service was added to the Dallas-Denison line. World War I brought more business—and runaway inflation which was aggravated by the severe postwar business slump. The TE began looking around for additional sources of revenue.

Much of the TE system was capable of handling line-haul railroad freight cars and, although many interurbans had scant success in winning interchange agreements with the reluctant steam roads, the TE overcame all opposition and on May 1, 1928, the first car of interline freight was handled—through an interchange set up at Italy, Texas, with the Missouri Pacific and the Katy. On-line freight was carried in a fleet of box motors converted from old passenger coaches, as well as in boxcars and other special purpose equipment.

The added revenue from freight came none too soon, for in the late 1920s and early 1930s the private automobile began siphoning off much of the line's passenger traffic. The arrival of the Great Depression (the last straw for many another interurban) further weakened the TE, and the company was placed in receivership in 1931. But the railroad fought back. One-man operation of cars reduced platform costs, but schedules were not drastically pruned as on other lines. In fact, the TE continued to be rather big business as electric railways went. When the receivership was terminated, in 1936, the TE had 464 employes and 973 stockholders.

One by one, the loss-making local street railways were dropped until only the Waco system remained. Dwindling oilfield activity prompted abandonment of the Corsicana branch in 1941, leaving the north-south mainline totaling 165 track miles. As it did to all public transportation systems, World War II gave Texas Electric a staggering rush of business; passengers increased from 606,000 in 1941 to 2,500,000 in 1945. Freight business boomed, too.

The bubble burst shortly after the end of World War II in 1945. As soon as gasoline rationing ended and it became possible once again to buy new autos, much of Texas Electric's passenger business evaporated and many runs were made with cars almost empty. Restrictions on trucking were eased, and the tonnage returned to the highways.

The TE had always been an exceptionally well-run railroad, always alert to the realities of its operational and economic environment. Economist George Hilton notes that although gross revenue fell from the 1921 high of more than $3 million the operating ratio stayed at about 60 throughout the twenties and the rate of return on investment more than 4 per cent, so the TE was probably one of the few interurbans that more or less justified its original investment. The interurban's board of directors, prudent realists, decided in 1948 that times had changed; that the TE had no future and should be abandoned before the last dime was spent. Permission was sought and secured, and the last car ran in the final hours of December 31, 1948.

WACO
317
2.37
FRONT ENTRANCE

In the beginning...

THE TEXAS ELECTRIC started life—as it ended it—with some uncommonly beautiful interurban cars. The 1912-era motorman was all business as he dolefully surveyed the photographer in this company publicity shot. The Pullman green cars looked rather somber, an effect heightened by the lighting and the contrasty film used in those days. Those double shank trolley poles are a mystery; perhaps somebody can explain what they were about. Photo from Charles A. Smallwood.

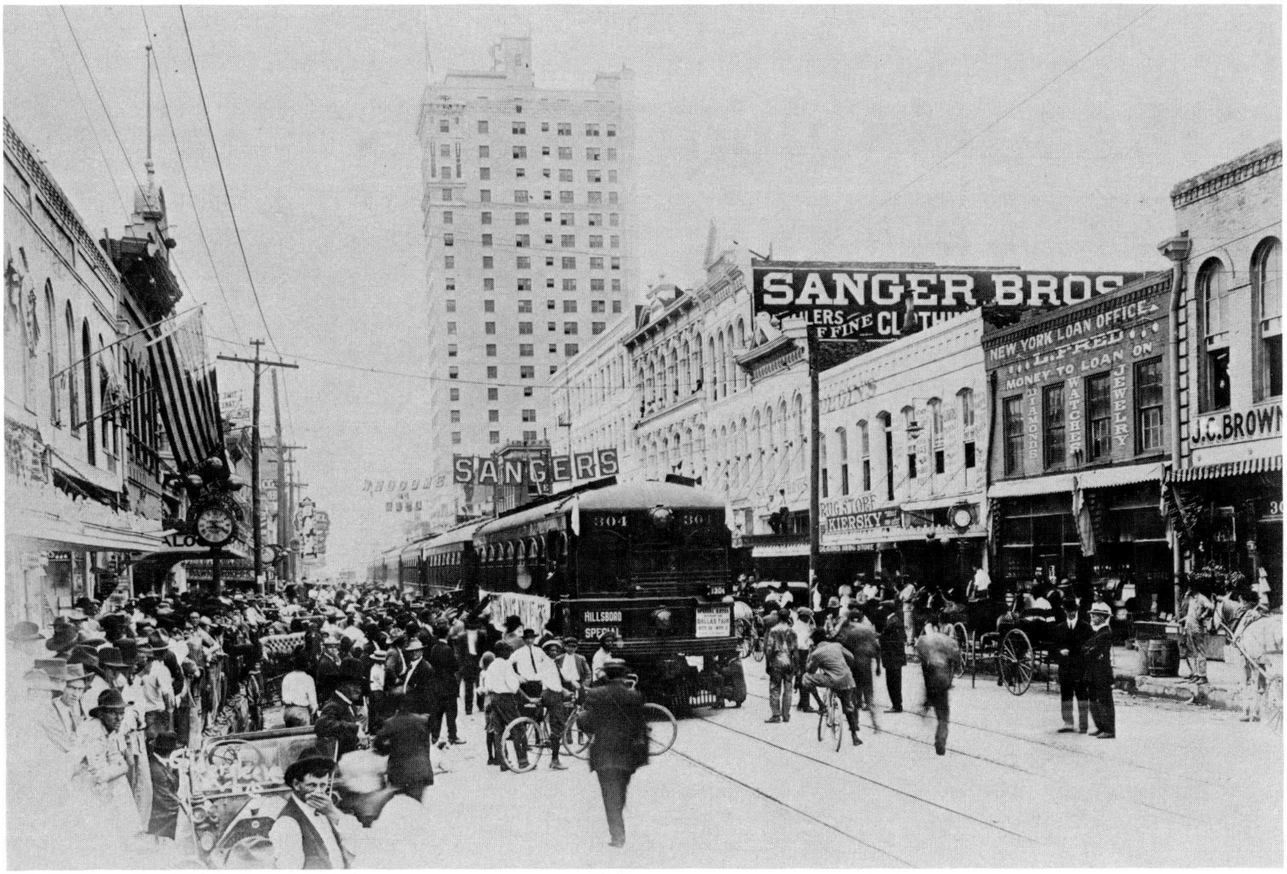
SANGER BROS
SANGERS
NEW YORK LOAN OFFICE
MONEY TO LOAN ON
DIAMONDS
WATCHES
JEWELRY
J.C. BROWN
KIERSKY
304
HILLSBORO SPECIAL

304
SOUTHERN
SPECIAL RATES

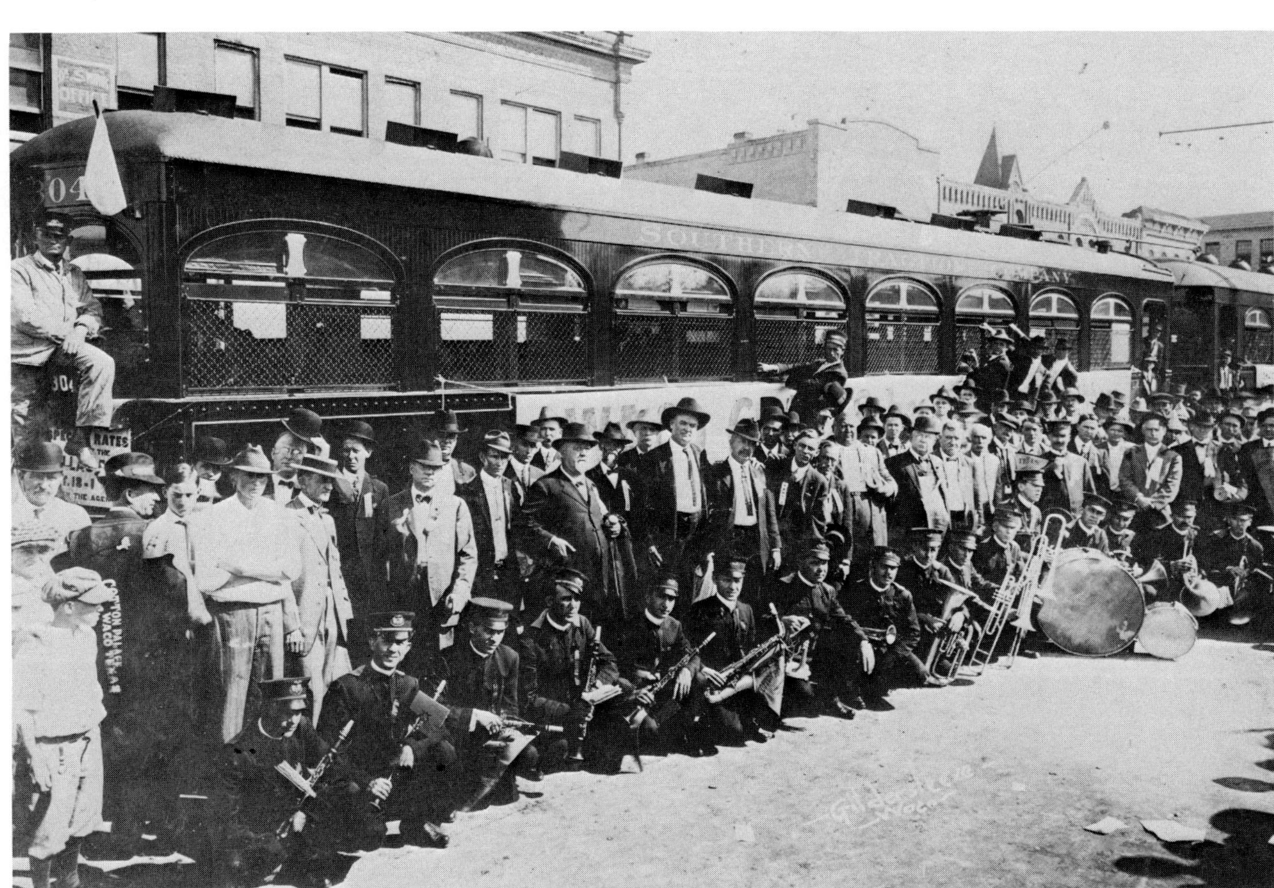

ANOTHER GOOD OLD DAYS SHOT. This one is at Monroe Shops late in the evening. Car 319 is headed for Corsicana as Limited Train No. 633 and is patiently waiting while the two high-level company officials have a conference. The train on the right carries white flags so it is a special movement. Photo from Charles A. Smallwood.

Top, opposite.

HERE IS A SIX-CAR TRAIN arriving in Waco on September 13, 1913, opening day of the line. Destination sign indicates that the train must have originated in Hillsboro, leading us to surmise that the line from Dallas to Hillsboro had been opened and operating previous to this time. Office building towering above the cars is the Amicable Life Insurance home office, then the tallest structure in Texas. C.V. Hess Collection.

Bottom, opposite.

OPENING DAY in Waco, 1913, complete with uniformed brass band. With a little imagination you can spot the original models for Burl Ives, Charles Coburn and the Texas Ranger. People look different now (or do they?) but the desire to be in the picture is still the same. This photo of car 304 was taken by a pioneer Waco photographer named Gildersleeve. C.V. Hess Collection.

A 151-Mile, 1200-Volt Line in Texas

This Catenary Line Gives High-Speed Service Between Dallas, Waco, Corsicana and Other Important Cities in a Rich Cotton Country—Three of the Seven Substations Have Three-Piece Motor-Generator Sets for Delivery of 600-Volt and 1200-Volt Current

Another long link in the chain of electric interurban railways radiating from Dallas, Tex., has been completed. This new line was built by the Southern Traction Company and forms a 151-mile extension to the Texas Traction Company's lines, making in all an electric railway system of approximately 250 miles. This is by far the longest electric line in Texas and it is also the longest one in the South.

Interurban railway construction in Texas began in 1900 with a 10½-mile line between Denison and Sherman. This was followed two years later by a 35-mile line between Dallas and Fort Worth, built by the Stone & Webster Management Association. The first interurban construction on a large scale, however, was started by the Texas Traction Company in 1906 when it began the laying of a 76-mile line between Dallas and Sherman.

During 1911 and 1912 the success of the first installations led to the construction of more than 230 miles of electric lines in the State, which included the Galveston-Houston Electric Railway, 50 miles long, and the Fort Worth Southern Traction Company, 32 miles long, both of which were started in 1911. In the following year the Southern Traction Company financed and commenced building its 151-mile extension, which was completed and put in operation in January, 1914.

THE ROUTE

This new 1200-volt line of the Southern Traction Company is made up of two sections, one extending from Dallas to Waco, 97.1 miles in length, and another from Dallas to Corsicana, a distance of 54 miles. Both of these divisions, along with the original line between Dallas and Sherman, Tex., traverse the heart of the great Black Land belt. This is the most densely populated and highly productive section of Texas. Within recent years Dallas has become the metropolis of the Southwest, being a railroad and business center as well as a distributing point for manufacturers' equipment and supplies for Texas and the extreme Southwest of the United States. Moreover, added impetus has been given to business prosperity in Texas by the approaching completion of the Panama Canal. With this in sight, many railroads have improved their terminals and bettered their roadbeds in order to facilitate the movement of freight to the Galveston seaboard.

A natural channel of travel exists between Dallas, Waxahachie, Hillsboro and Waco, as well as between Dallas and Corsicana, each being the county seat of a rich cotton-producing territory. In fact, Waxahachie is said to be the largest inland cotton market in the world. Taking advantage of this condition, as well as the infrequent service furnished by steam roads between the points named, the Southern Traction Company was financed locally and undertook the construction of the new electric lines.

Another feature which helps to make electric interurban railway construction and operation profitable in Texas is the fact that the legal fare is 3 cents per mile. In addition, interurban lines do not carry bulk freight, but engage in an extensive first and second-class express business with rates fixed a little less than those charged by old-line express companies. Earnings which would be considered phenomenal in other parts of the United States are obtained by Texas electric railways. Few of them earn less than 40 cents per car-mile, with an hourly passenger service and at least two or three express trains each way daily.

Summer in Texas lasts approximately ten months of the year, during which period people travel by the electric line almost exclusively in order to be free from the dirt and dust incident to steam railroad travel. This tendency has been clearly demonstrated on the line between Dallas and Fort Worth, where a steam railroad between the same points proceeded to give very frequent service at rates far below the least the electric lines could afford to charge. Despite this the travel between these two cities went the electric way almost exclusively, and in time the steam railroad had to abandon its local competitive service.

CONSTRUCTION FEATURES

Topographical conditions in the territory traversed were not ideal for the construction of a first-class interurban railway at least cost for grading, while the undulating black earth and clay hills made the grading quantities per mile quite heavy. However, these cuts and fills through the gently rolling, highly productive

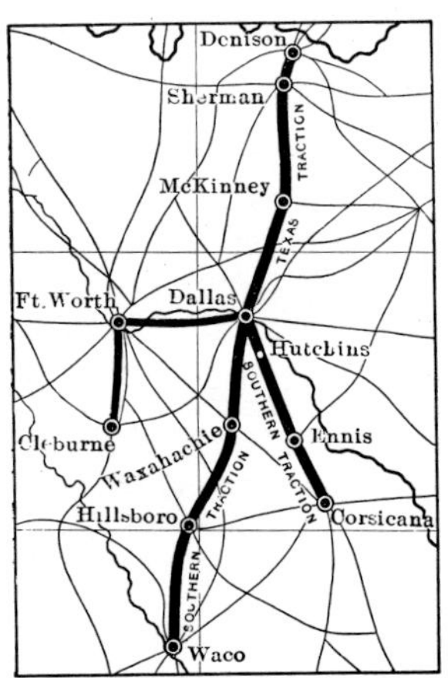

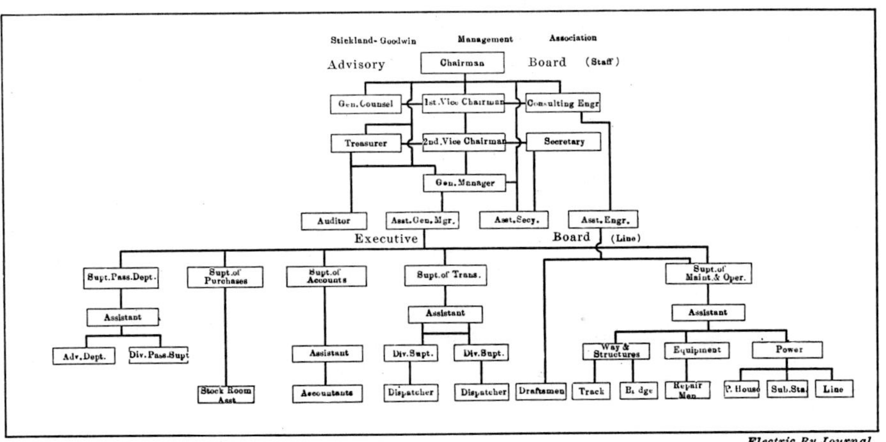

Electric Ry Journal

SOUTHERN TRACTION—CHART OF CONSOLIDATED MANAGEMENT SOUTHERN & TEXAS TRACTION COMPANIES

SOUTHERN TRACTION—CEDAR CREEK BALLAST DECK VIADUCT NEAR DALLAS

SOUTHERN TRACTION—BRAZOS RIVER BRIDGE

agricultural country made the new interurban line an interesting and picturesque one to the traveler. On the other hand, profiting by experience in electric railway construction since 1900, the Southern Traction Company provided a high-speed roadbed with a maximum grade of 2 per cent outside of the city streets and a maximum curvature of 6 deg. except where governed by streets. Of the total mileage built 91½ per cent is tangent track.

A private right-of-way varying in width from 80 ft. to 100 ft., depending upon the amount necessary to complete the grading economically, was purchased outside the cities. Additional widths were acquired at points where station sites were desired, or to provide sidings. This right-of-way is inclosed with a five-wire Osage-orange post fence with wing fences and cattle guards at all highway crossings. The standard roadway section is 16-ft. wide on embankments and 24 ft. in cuts, with a liberal allowance for shrinkage so that the seasoned embankment will remain full width. On embankments the slope is 1½ to 1, and in excavation it varies from ¼ to 1 to 1 to 1, depending upon soil conditions. The highest fill is at a point near Dallas over a 15-ft. concrete arch culvert, where the top embankment is 65 ft. above the floor of the culvert.

As mentioned heretofore, this extension comprises 151 miles of main line track, 20 miles of which, namely, between Dallas and Waxahachie, was acquired from the Stone & Webster Management Association. In addition, the completed line includes about 2 miles of second track and approximately 5 miles of sidings. The standard type of construction of all these tracks includes 6-in. x 8-in. x 8-ft. seasoned white oak ties, spaced seventeen ties to a 33-ft. rail. The ties were laid on 6 in. of gravel ballast except in paved streets, where 6 in. of concrete was placed under the ties. All gravel was taken from the railway's pits at Waco and Hutchins. Approximately 80 miles of the main-line track was built with 80-lb. A. S. C. E. rail and the remainder, except 5 miles in city streets, was built of 70-lb. A. S. C. E. rail. All turnouts from the main track are No. 9, with a 77.5-ft. lead laid on white oak switch ties cut to length, and equipped with medium height Buda switch stands. Practically all sidings were constructed with stub-ends; when the subgrade has thoroughly seasoned they will be double-ended.

BRIDGES AND STRUCTURES

In all, the construction of this new line comprises eighteen steel bridges or steel viaducts having a total length of 3513 ft. The longest single span was placed over the Brazos River at Waco, being 450 ft. in length and forming three 150-ft. spans. The longest viaduct, 1454 ft., was built at a grade separation which carries the interurban line over the main line and side tracks of two steam railroads at Waxahachie. All steel bridges and viaducts were designed to carry Cooper's E-30 loading. Probably the most interesting piece of bridge construction was encountered in building the

SOUTHERN TRACTION—VIADUCT AT WAXAHACHIE

SOUTHERN TRACTION—INTERIOR OF PASSENGER MOTOR CAR

piers for the Brazos River bridge. At this point caissons were necessary to carry on the pier excavation. These were constructed of reinforced concrete with 12-in. walls, beveled at the bottom to form a cutting edge so that they would settle readily as the excavation progressed. The complete reinforced-concrete caissons were about 16 ft. in height, extending from bedrock to the bed of the river. In order to conduct the excavating to advantage, however, the caissons were built in several sections. When bedrock was reached the bottom was sealed, after which the open caisson was used as a form for the concrete piers.

Concrete structures included two reinforced-concrete ballast-rock trestles, one 660 ft. long and another 340 ft. long. Both of these structures were required just south of Dallas, and are combination reinforced-concrete, deck-girder, ballast-deck structures, the former structure, however, supported on concrete piers and the latter structure supported on two-column bents and four-column towers alternately spaced along the length of the structure. A number of other waterways were provided with concrete arches, two of which are noteworthy, one being a 50-ft. reinforced-concrete arch and the other a 40-ft. arch. All reinforced-concrete structures were designed for Cooper's E-40 loading.

In several instances the size of the opening was questionable, and rather than run any risk of future renewals by building permanent structures, wooden-pile trestles were provided. These, it was believed, would give sufficient life to enable the engineers to study conditions accurately and replace them with permanent structures when renewals were necessary. In fact, the size of these trestle openings were severely tested during the record floods in December, 1913. All trestles withstood these floods without damage, and in each instance it was demonstrated that the large temporary openings provided were necessary. In all, 11,147 ft., or 2.1 miles, of wooden-pile trestle were constructed on this new line. Small openings, namely, those between 12 in. and 48 in. in size, were supplied by non-corrosive corrugated culverts.

At three points where steam railroads were crossed, topographical conditions were such as to make grade separation exceedingly expensive. At these points the crossings were installed at grade and were protected by derails on each side of the steam railroad. The derails are operated by an interlocking device designed so that the conductor may readily close them. The locking-bed elements, however, are so arranged that the derail cannot be closed until after the danger signals have been set on the steam line, and these signals cannot be dropped to the danger position if a train is within 2000 ft. of the crossing. This locking feature is controlled by a clock set for a thirty second release.

ENERGY GENERATION AND DISTRIBUTION

Energy for this new line is supplied at 2300 volts, sixty cycles by the Texas Power & Light Company, an organization controlled by the same holding company as the one which operates the interurban line. At present this energy is transmitted from the power and light company's Fort Worth station, but the larger portion of this load will ultimately be transferred to a new generating station now under construction at Waco. Energy is transmitted to six substations, including three terminal and three intermediate stations, located in the principal cities on the two divisions of the road. Each substation feeds a trolley section slightly in excess of 25 miles in length.

The three terminal substations are situated at Mon-

SOUTHERN TRACTION—PASSENGER MOTOR CAR WITH TRAILER

SOUTHERN TRACTION—WORK CAR

roe, a suburb of Dallas, Corsicana and Waco. Each is equipped with two 400-kw motor-generator three-piece sets, designed to deliver both 600 volts and 1200 volts d.c. to the trolley line, the lower voltage being necessary to comply with the ordinances of Dallas, Corsicana and Waco.

The three intermediate substations are located at Waxahachie, Hillsboro and Ennis. Each has one 400-kw motor-generator two-piece set, designed to deliver only 1200 volts d.c. In addition to the three intermediate substations, a portable substation has been purchased for use in cases of emergency.

As shown in one of the accompanying illustrations, the substations are housed in fireproof brick and concrete buildings, 40 ft. x 50 ft. in plan, with a clear inside height of 15 ft. The transmission lines enter the substation by way of a structural-steel terminal tower formed of four built-up tower posts which support the terminal insulator racks. From this point the transmission lines connect into transformers located in the space defined by the four tower posts, and lead from there to the substation by way of a small transmission bracket located on the roof, and roof insulators. The out-door substation equipment is enclosed with a high-woven wire fence as a safety measure.

OVERHEAD CONSTRUCTION

All trolley construction, except that on city streets, is of the catenary type, nine-point suspension carried on mast-arms. It is supported on 9-in. top, 35-ft. Idaho cedar poles spaced at 150-ft. intervals on tangent track, and at closer intervals on curves. The mast-arms are of the usual structural T-beam section, 9 ft. in length, provided with special end-castings at feeder taps and a long bracket steady brace at frequent intervals. Clearance between the top of rail and trolley are fixed at 19 ft. Feeder taps are supplied five to each mile, and lightning arresters at the same interval.

The high-tension transmission line is carried on steel towers along the company's right-of-way, except through the cities, where it was necessary to purchase a private right-of-way around them. This tower line follows the right-of-way from Waco to Waxahachie and from Ferris to Trinity Heights. It was built primarily

SOUTHERN TRACTION—COMBINATION LINE AND WORK CAR

to serve a number of lighting and power properties in the cities and villages in this territory. From Ferris to Corsicana the transmission line is carried on wooden poles along with the trolley wire.

On city streets the overhead construction is changed to a simple trolley on span wires. Here also compressed, concealed rail bonds are provided in place of the brazed bond used in open-track construction. In addition to these five crossbonds are installed in each mile and special No. 0000 long bonds provided around switches and railroad crossings. Overhead construction on the bridges and viaducts, where the spans were too long and too high to permit poles to be set in the ground, was provided by setting the poles on structural-steel brackets projecting from the piers and towers. The butt of the pole was set on the bracket and it was tied in just below the bridge deck level by a structural-steel bracket designed to hold the pole rigidly in position. Several typical overhead construction installations are shown in the accompanying illustrations.

Two complete metallic telephone circuits are also carried on cross-arms set immediately below the mast-arms. These were provided for a telephone-selector system furnished by the Western Electric Company. The telephone circuits are No. 10 copper wire mounted on porcelain insulators and each telephone is protected from the high-trolley voltage by a small transformer. Both of these telephone lines are used for train dispatching; a third circuit is to be added and used as a commercial line when required.

REPAIR SHOPS AND ROLLING STOCK

General repair shops are now being constructed at Monroe, a suburb just south of Dallas, and at the junction point of the lines to Waco and Corsicana. All heavy general repair work for the new line as well as the lines of the Texas Traction Company north of Dallas will be concentrated at this point. Ordinary running repairs necessary to maintain schedules on the Dallas-Sherman line will be done at the repair shop at McKinney, where all repair work is being handled until the new general repair shops are completed.

SOUTHERN TRACTION—STANDARD SUBSTATION

SOUTHERN TRACTION—OVERHEAD ON TANGENT

A complete equipment of rolling stock including passenger, express and work cars was purchased for this line, and is now in service. This list included twenty-two passenger motor cars built by the St. Louis Car Company, six express motor cars, ten passenger trail cars, two express trail cars and two motor work cars furnished by the American Car Company. All of these cars were built with underframes of composite construction, except the motor passenger cars, which are of semi-steel. The cars are finished in golden oak with tan grain leather upholstered seats. All cars were designed for high-speed. The principal general dimensions of the motor passenger cars are as follows: Over-all length, 53 ft. 6 in.; over-all width, 9 ft.; seating capacity, fifty-six passengers. The electrical equipment in these cars includes four GE-225 motors arranged for single-end control. Each car has a switch to permit full speed operation on either 600 volts or 1200 volts.

The ten passenger trail cars were also designed for high-speed interurban service, and to be coupled in trains of two or more cars each. Each side of the car is framed for seven pairs of double windows with oval-top sashes. The bulkheads at each end are fitted with single sliding doors, which, together with the end windows, are removable in hot weather. The express motor and trail cars are practically identical in construction with the passenger trail cars, except that they are designed for a carrying capacity of 40,000 lb.

SOUTHERN TRACTION—WARNING SIGNS ON BRIDGES

The combination work and line cars also have composite underframes similar to the express motor and trail cars, except for minor changes in size of the steel members. These cars were designed to carry a distributed load of 40 tons at high speed, and the principal dimensions are as follows: Work car: Length over bumpers, 50 ft.; width over sills, 8 ft. 4½ in.; width of cab, 5 ft.; length of cab, 7 ft.; wheelbase, 6 ft. 6 in.; diameter of wheels, 37 in., and Brill trucks 27-MCB-3 with 100 hp GE-225 motors.

The dimensions of the combination work and line car: Length over bumpers, 50 ft.; length of body over cab, 24 ft. 6 in.; width over sills, 8 ft. 4¼ in.; extreme width, 9 ft.; height from track to underside of side sills, 43 in.; height from rail over trolley boards, 14 ft. 10½ in.; height from bottom of sill to top roof of car, 8 ft. 6½ in.; Brill trucks 27-MCB-3 and GE-225 motors. Views of these cars are shown in the illustrations.

GENERAL

The Southern Traction Company was promoted and financed by J. F. Strickland, its president. Its opening was made an auspicious occasion with celebrations in all the important cities along the line. Much stock was sold locally, consequently there was a personal interest in the success of its operation. The road is known as the "Home Interurban." The actual construction was done by the Southern Engineering & Construction Company, of Dallas, of which Burr Martin is president and Luther Dean is vice-president and chief engineer. The operation of this new line, as well as that of the Texas Traction Company, is under the direction of R. B. Stichter, general manager.

The Canadian Radial Electric Railway Act

In a long report which he has made to the Bureau of Foreign and Domestic Commerce of the Department of Commerce of the United States on commercial and economic conditions in Ontario, Consul Julius D. Dreher at Toronto, Canada, says in referring to electric railway progress and to the extension of the radial electric railway:

"The street and rural electric railways in the Dominion have a total first main track mileage of 1357, or, including second main track mileage, a total of 1727 miles. Of the former total, Ontario lines have 543 miles, or 40 per cent, and of the latter 659 miles, or 38 per cent. Of the total capitalization of $141,235,631 the lines in Ontario have $44,591,296, or 31.6 per cent, and of the total net income for the year ended June 30, 1913, amounting to $6,612,575, Ontario lines made $2,710,375, or 41 per cent, which was a net profit of 6.1 per cent on the total capital invested in Ontario lines. Only three of these lines showed a deficit last year, the aggregate loss being $34,197. It is expected that the mileage of rural car lines will be considerably increased in the near future.

"In April last the Dominion Parliament passed an act conferring further powers on the Hydroelectric Commission in order to promote the building of radial, or interurban electric railways. Under the provisions of this act the commission will construct, equip and operate these lines for the benefit and at the expense of the municipalities. The railways will be built with money secured by issues of bonds by the Hydroelectric Commission, guaranteed by the Province. The government will in turn be protected by requiring the municipalities to deposit with the commission debentures covering the expenditure made. The interest, sinking fund, or possible deficits will be met by the municipalities interested. The bonds covering construction will be extended over a period of fifty years, a provision calculated to lighten the burden upon the enterprise, and in order to tide over the first ten years, when the roads are getting under way, the municipalities will not be required to pay sinking fund charges at all.

"As an added protection for the commission, it is provided that where a municipality defaults on its interest or sinking-fund payments the commission shall have the right to go on the market and sell the debentures of that municipality to make up the deficiency. Where the debentures fail to produce the necessary amount the municipalities can still be made liable for any amount still due the commission, as its bonds will be a first mortgage upon the railway property.

"The responsibility for entering upon a radial railway project lies entirely with the municipalities. The commission is empowered to enter into a contract with one or more municipalities, with the approval of the Lieutenant-Governor in council. The agreement or contract must then be submitted to the electors qualified to vote upon money by-laws."

For electrification of railways in Japan the sum of $1,250,000 has been included in the budget for the current year of the Japanese Imperial Railway Board.

NOT AN AUTOMOBILE is in sight on this hot June 30, 1908 day as the "Stockholders Special," operated with at least five cars, stands on Kentucky Street in McKinney on the Dallas-Sherman-Denison line of the Texas Traction Co. Full service began the next day. C.V. Hess Collection.

MYSTERY CAR 39, shown at the American Car and Foundry Co. Jeffersonville, Ind., plant may have seen a short period of service in Texas but no on-the-property shots of this trailer have been located. David J. Williams III Collection.

WAXAHACHIE's FAMOUS 1,200-volt cars 95, 96 and 97 were really rare lightweights. Texas Electric planned it that way when they took over the mule car system to save putting in a 600v substation and a 600v section right in the middle of their 1,200v main-line through the city. "West End" was one of three local lines. Other lines were "East End" and "University." The gent in the picture, warming his hand with a pipe, is unknown to us—he could have been the mayor! Photo from Charles A. Smallwood.

EARLY POST CARD stressed the bucolic nature of the Texas Electric route. (I)

THE WHOLE GANG IS HERE! The place is Waxahachie, October 3, 1915, on the east side of the station. Man with the bowtie, suspenders and bowler hat is the agent; we can assume the others are crew and express handlers. Motorman, third from left—he with the big gloves. Express motor 500 is only a couple of years old and still has its original gold lettering and lining and two bull's-eye carbon-arc lamps. It's noon which accounts for the man in front munching on an apple while his "brown bag" is stuffed into his overcoat pocket. Train No. 510 is southbound toward Waco. By the early 1930s this run had been downgraded to a trailer on Train 221. C.V. Hess Collection.

THE YEAR IS 1915 and everybody took time out to have his picture taken. This Stone & Webster-type car has all the refinements of that period: two-man operation, horn-type intake ventilators above platform roofs, capable of multiple unit operation and only one trolley pole. Location was 10th & Colcord in Waco. The motorman is G.C. Gibson and the conductor is Jim Clark. From Leroy Sweetland, original owned by motorman Gibson 1967.

AN EARLY 1920s picture of the Waco service crew proudly posing with one of their charges just in from Dallas. This was a local–it made all the stops while limiteds paused only at Waxahachie, Italy and Hillsboro on flag. In the good old days, the locals ran on the hour and the limiteds on the half hour. C.V. Hess Collection.

Tickets, please

.05	DALLAS	1
	Lisbon	TAX
10	Glendale	
.15		2
.20	Henry	3
.25	Waverly	4
.30	LANCASTER	5
.35	Ardmore	6
.40	RED OAK	7
.45	STERRETT	8
.50	Harrison	9
.55	Hilcrest	10
.60	WAXAHACHIE	11
.65	Pierce	12
.70	Stroud	13
.75	Coleman	14
.80	FORRESTON	15
.85	Watson	16
.90	ITALY	17
.95	Dunlap	18
1.00	MILFORD	19
1.05	McDaniel	20
1.10	Wear	21
1.15	Woodall	22
1.20	Ellington	23
1.25	Bond	24
1.30	HILLSBORO	25
1.35	Scott	26
1.40	Conover	27
1.45	Duff	28
1.50	ABBOTT	29
1.55	Glasgow	30
1.60	WEST	31
1.65	Casey	32
1.70	Sanger	33
1.75	Drake	3/
1.80	Long	3
1.85	akeview	
1.90	Ralph	
1.95	CO	
	CHILD	

57990

Form 72

...ELECTRIC RAILWAY COMPANY ...ined as evidence of fare paid. Good only for one continu... ...DEEMABLE. Punch marks indicate the stations ... ...nt thereof. If more than two stations are

.05		TAX
	DALLAS	1
	Lovers Lane	
.10	Works	
.15	VICKERY	2
.20	Kirkland	3
.25	Huffhines	4
.30	RICHARDSON	5
.35	Roller	6
.40	PLANO	7
.45	Jasper	8
.50	ALLEN	9
.55	Murray	10
.60	Waddill	11
.65	McKINNEY	12
.70	Wilson	13
.75	Heard	14
.80	MELISSA	15
.85	Williams	16
.90	ANNA	17
.95	Fulton	18
1.00	VAN ALSTYNE	19
1.05	Dixie	20
1.10	HOWE	21
1.15	Holt	22
1.20	Dodson	23
1.25	Payne	24
1.30	SHERMAN	25
1.35	Highland	26
1.40	Woodlake	27
1.45	Willow Grove	28
1.50	DENISON	29
	CHILD	

255333

Form 70

TEXAS ELECTRIC RAILWAY COMPANY

PASSENGER'S RECEIPT. To be retained as evidence of fare paid. Good only for one continuous trip between stations punched. NOT REDEEMABLE. Punch marks indicate the stations between which fare has been paid, and the amount thereof. If more than two stations are punched this receipt is void.

Passengers are requested to purchase tickets before boarding cars. Your Local Agent will appreciate it as it will improve his standing. The operator will appreciate it as it lessens his labors.

General Superintendent

General Passenger Agent

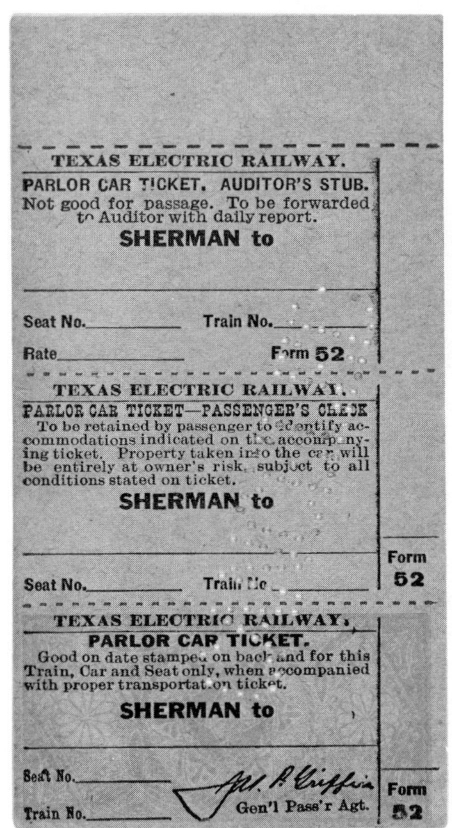
TEXAS ELECTRIC RAILWAY.
PARLOR CAR TICKET. AUDITOR'S STUB.
Not good for passage. To be forwarded to Auditor with daily report.
SHERMAN to

Seat No.________ Train No.________
Rate________ Form 52

TEXAS ELECTRIC RAILWAY.
PARLOR CAR TICKET—PASSENGER'S CHECK
To be retained by passenger to identify accommodations indicated on the accompanying ticket. Property taken into the car will be entirely at owner's risk, subject to all conditions stated on ticket.
SHERMAN to

Seat No.________ Train No.________
Form 52

TEXAS ELECTRIC RAILWAY.
PARLOR CAR TICKET.
Good on date stamped on back and for this Train, Car and Seat only, when accompanied with proper transportation ticket.
SHERMAN to

Seat No.________
Train No.________
Gen'l Pass'r Agt.
Form 52

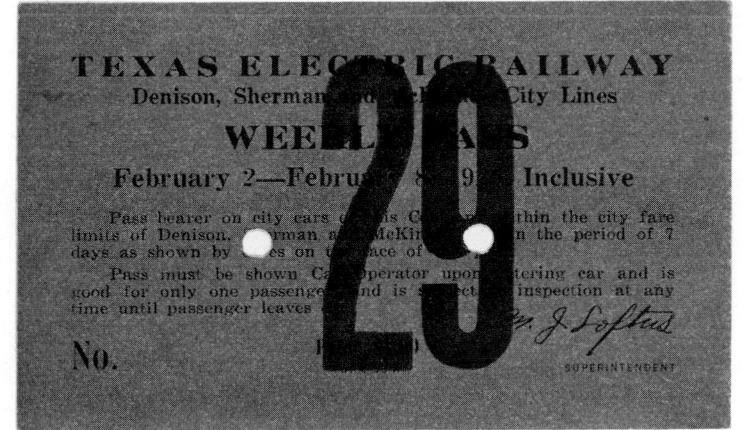
TEXAS ELECTRIC RAILWAY
Denison, Sherman ... City Lines
WEE...
February 2—Febru... 8 ... 9... Inclusive
Pass bearer on city cars ... within the city fare limits of Denison, ...rman a... McKin... in the period of 7 days as shown by ...es on ... face of ...
Pass must be shown Ca... Operator upon entering car and is good for only one passenger and is ... inspection at any time until passenger leaves ...
No.
29
SUPERINTENDENT

From "Electric Traction," CVH collection.

It paid to advertise

April 24, 1926

Texas Electric Advertises for Increased Business

PROVISION for more extended advertising was made in an increased budget allowance for the purpose voted for 1926 by the directors of the Texas Electric Railway, Dallas, Tex. This work has been promptly started and several pieces of newspaper advertising copy now being used are shown on this page.

This advertising is handled by means of a company advertising council, which meets frequently to plan the type and kind of advertising for the month ahead. Rough copy and advertising ideas that are developed by the council are turned over to one of the Dallas advertising agencies for the preparation of final copy. The council again meets to approve this before it actually appears in the newspapers.

Under this plan the Texas Electric Railway will use a great deal of daily and weekly newspaper space in the papers of the local communities. It is also planned to use car cards in the cars and on the dash racks of the cars, as well as to use billboards, art posters, blotters, mailing cards, etc.

To advertise the express business the company has recently painted its express cars in the spectacular manner illustrated. The body color is a very bright blue, the large lettering being in gold, the "Safe, Sure, Saving" in white, the monogram in the standard red with white letters, and the heart-shaped background for the map of the Texas Electric Railway in white. The Texas Electric route is shown in red, while connecting traction lines are shown in black.

Newspapers and Freight Cars Are Used by the Texas Electric Railway to Advertise for More Business

Below, new express car of the Texas Electric Railway. Several of these cars have been constructed in the company's shops and have been painted in very striking colors. They attract attention and will be used as a traveling billboard.

At right, samples of newspaper advertising used in the campaign recently started for more business by the Texas Electric Railway.

Riding in style...

Parlor Cars

Service deLuxe

SCHEDULE

Lv. Denison	7:00 am	3:00 pm
Lv. Sherman	7:35 am	3:35 pm
Ar. Dallas	10:00 am	6:00 pm
Lv. Dallas	11:00 am	7:00 pm
Ar. Sherman	1:27 pm	9:27 pm
Ar. Denison	1:55 pm	9:55 pm

Parlor Cars leave Dallas for Waco 11:30 am. and 7:30 pm.

Roomy, Comfortable Chairs of latest Parlor Car type. Smoking and Observation Compartments.

N. C. CALVERT, D. P. A., Denison C. B. ANDERSON, Agent, Sherman

THIS PROBABLY WAS POSED for a company postcard, what with the logo superimposed on the lower left. Combine semisteel 313 ended up as car 314 to get away from the jinx numeral. This St. Louis Car product could run 600 and 1,200 volts. Dash light on left front was removed before very long. Photo from Charles A. Smallwood.

The TE in its prime

GEORGE SIDING, between Howe and Van Alstyne, was one of the customary meeting places for TE trains in the late 1930s and early 1940s. Car 367 is train No. 7 which left Denison at 8:00AM and is meeting northbound train No. 6 just a little after nine o'clock. Looks like the operators are passing the toolbox as well as the time of day. Those blue serge uniforms could pick up a high shine in those days! (Can you imagine a doubleknit interurban uniform?) Looks like they have the luxury of a switch tender, judging by the gent in overalls standing in the center background. This fine photo was made on April 9, 1940, by Charles D. Savage.

FINE SHOT of the Waco "Blue Bonnet" also taken by Charles Savage on April 9, 1940. Shown here is the Trinity Heights trestle with motor 312 at speed. This car would soon be rebuilt to finish out its years at second 368. Overhead collector wire above this single-track trestle has two wires; one for each direction of travel to avoid depoling accidents by eliminating overhead frogs at each end. If you look sharp you can see a couple of Mr. Metzger's cows in the background through one of the arches—also the Metzger Dairy barn. Ah, serenity!

ANOTHER ONE OF THOSE April 9, 1940 Savage photos depicts this Classic Interurban Scene. Train No. 623 is stopped in the middle of the street in downtown Ennis. It looks like the station agent is getting ready to heave a pouch of express aboard this big red and white car. The operator inside the cab is leaning over to retrieve something from the floor. One of those dark green (but faded) 600-series (ex-parlor) express cars is attached. It's just about 2 o'clock in the afternoon and the car is due in Corsicana at 2:30PM. (CDS)

HERE'S A RARE SHOT of a special movement in Hillsboro. White marker flags advertise the extra status of car 328. Probably a railfan charter as at least three camera bugs are visible in the right-hand side background. Hillsboro Interurban Station is just out of the picture's extreme right, while the county courthouse tower stands guard over the proceedings. The 328 was a honey. It was fast, quiet, efficient and handled on the road at high speeds much better than the older cars. There were four of these dandies: 325-328 made by St. Louis. They looked taller than the other cars—and they were by

JUST OUT OF DALLAS, Car 313 poses for the cameraman on April 10, 1940. This slick-looking car was once a combine as the extra row of rivets on the left front side attests. For one-manning, operators' controls and seat were moved to the left front side from the original right front window. This made room for end loading and exiting of passengers. Note oval handle on right side of the stepwell—that's the switch throw rod used in city track running. No. 313 became second No. 314 during the next rebuilding. What about first 314? Oh yes, it became freight motor 902. Besides, 313 is an unlucky number and Texas Electric was somewhat superstitious. Photo by Charles D. Savage.

WITH SPARE TROLLEY POLE much in evidence, TE 307 negotiates overpass spanning the Missouri-Kansas-Texas tracks near Dallas on May 21, 1946. There are plenty of weeds in this photo, but not many on either the TE or Katy right-of-way. Railroads—even interurban railroads—had more pride (and affluence) in those days. Photo by Charles D. Savage.

TEXAS ELECTRIC'S ENTRY in the Interurban Glamor Derby—"Old Glory" itself. This handsome Charles Smallwood photo shows the 319 at rest in the Dallas Interurban Terminal. Judging from the number of photos made of 319, it is an all-time favorite—the Texas Division ERA files contain at least 10 different shots. Study this photogenic Goliath a bit. It has Dallas "Blue Bonnet" markings, radial coupler, air hose, both style headlights, step well, air whistle on the roof, arch windows and an "ad" that brags that "the Safest Highway in North Texas is the Interurban Route." What more could the serious traveller or admiring railfan (if there were any in days of yore) want?

HAVING JUST ROLLED off the Trinity River viaduct, southbound 327 running as train No. 223 makes the customary stop just beyond the junction of the Seventh St. Dallas Railway carline. The building to the left, according to Walter Donalson, is a Dallas Railway & Terminal dispatchers office and the man sitting on the bench is the DS himself. A clerk is recording the train movement. At this point TE train 223 is still on street railway trackage and won't reach TE home iron for another three blocks. It's 1948 and time is about to run out on all this tractional activity. Photo by Robert P. Townley.

HOW DO YOU LIKE these swinging R.R. warning signals? Nothing like them nowadays! The operator of train 16, having made the required stop, has notched it up to get rolling and is now coasting across the diamond. That gal standing next to him must have asked him a question as he seems to be scratching his head for an answer. No. 351 was ex-No. 2 and was the first RPO but was remodeled back to coach form. August, 1948. Photo by Robert P. Townley.

On the lone prairie...

AS EVENING SHADOWS LENGTHEN, Train 232 holds the main on its mid-1940s run Waco to Dallas. If they are on the timecard, this scene is near Elm Mott and the meet will be with southbound train 225. This bleak-looking area was called Blue Siding. It's about 5:20PM—late enough to use the upper headlight but not dark enough for the lower bull's-eye lamp. Step lights punctuate the indigo mood of this lonesome prairie setting. (TERA)

RAILWAY POST OFFICE car 360 (ex-No. 11) is stopped a short distance out of Denison to let a trackworker put something aboard the regular evening mail train No. 21. The train left the terminal at 5:30PM but this is August (1948) so there is plenty of Texas sunshine left. In fact, it will still be daylight when they arrive in Dallas at 8:27PM. Photo by Robert P. Townley.

SOUTHBOUND TRAIN 11, motor 365, is meeting a northbound train on the Dallas-Denison line. The northbound will be train 12 scheduled to meet No. 11 around 12:48PM. From this we can deduce that this passing siding is somewhere in the vicinity of Anna or Melissa. August, 1948. Photo by Robert P. Townley.

HERE WE ARE AT ASH, Texas. And where is that, you say? Well, partner, it's between Stroud and Pierce, south of Waxahachie, that's where. No. 308 as Train 217 holds the main while waiting for a midmorning meet with a northbound movement. At each siding or passing turnout there was a phone booth where trainmen called for orders if the regular schedule was interrupted. This photo was taken on September 6, 1948, and the weeds will have this right-of-way all to themselves in just a few months. Photo by Anthony Kaisak.

THIS 800-FOOT TRESTLE across two railroads and Waxahachie Creek was a favorite of the trolley photographers. Catch a car on this 40-foot-high edifice and you had the makings of a fine traction picture. Car is southbound, just out of the downtown area. Waxahachie, by the way, is an Indian word meaning cow or buffalo creek. (I)

MOTORMAN's VIEW on the Corsicana line, taken February 2, 1941, just two days before abandonment. Scene is a few miles beyond Webb Switch. The town of Hutchins is in the distance. Even as the end neared, that track looks pretty well-groomed. (I)

NOW WE SEE SECOND (or is it third) No. 316 as Train 219 on the passenger loading track southbound at Abbott. Timecard says it should be 11:44AM and will reach Waco at 12:25. Just visible in the background is the cotton loading dock with the customary wooden barrel of water for fire protection. This freight siding stub-ended at the station. Photo from M.D. McCarter.

TROUBLE FROM THE SKIES MAY BE BREWING. This view, somewhere on the Waco line, caused P.C. McPherson J former TE employe, to remark: "Storms were numerous along this route. Many nights the wind would blow 50 miles hour all night long. Seemed like they originated in the area around Italy, and just tried to wreck the line. Next day li crews were out replacing poles and communications. It happened all the time." Occasionally, such clouds spawned deat dealing tornado twisters. Life along the Texas Electric wasn't always humdrum by any means. (TERA)

And in the busy terminal

TEXAS ELECTRIC SERVED (in addition to Big D) several sizable cities and towns, including Waco, Sherman and Denison. Down through the years, the TE terminals and stations in its cities witnessed the bustle of millions of passengers governed by the rhythmical cycle of the arrival and departure of the interurban cars. The bus stations in these towns, today, seem a lot less hectic by comparison. Train No. 14 is now in Sherman and the time is 3:30PM. Next stop is Denison at 4:02PM. The shortened version of a Red Cap leaning on the coupler must be trying to keep No. 310 from rolling forward. Photo by Robert P. Townley.

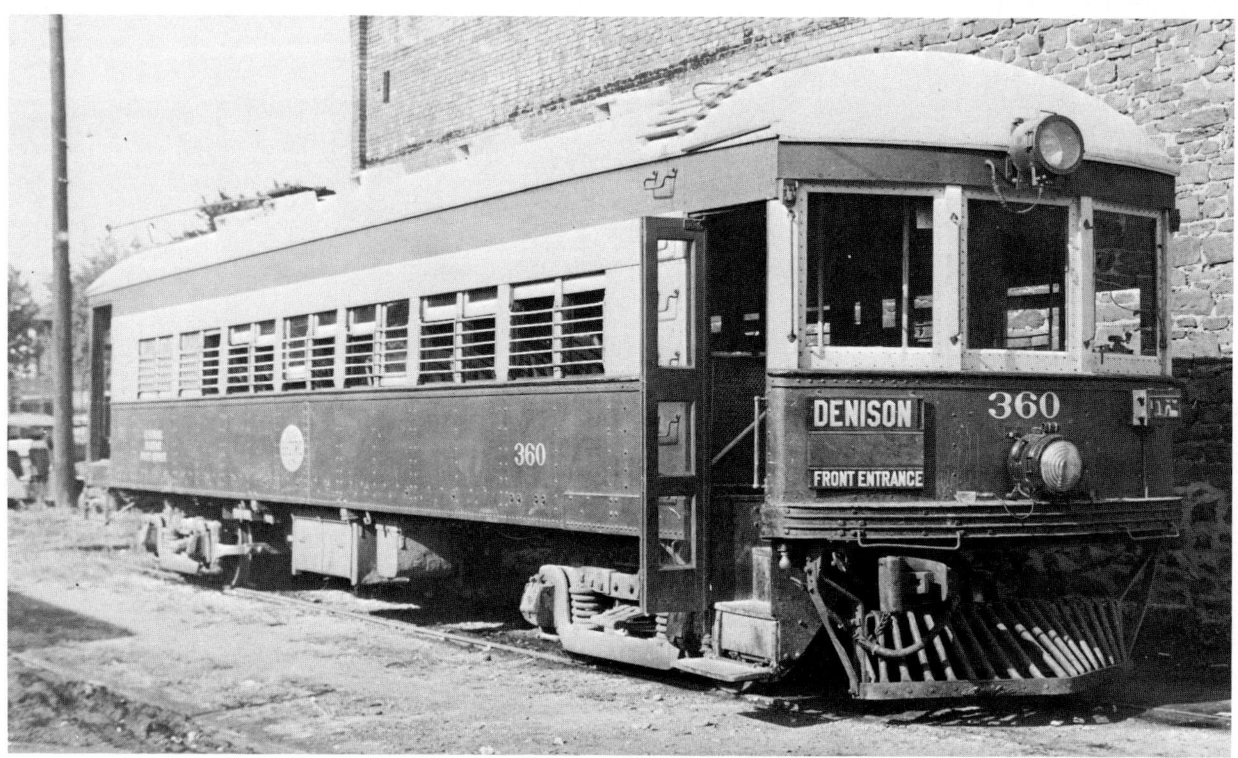

THE MORNING MAIL TRAIN, resting at Denison after its run from Dallas, has been idling in the August heat since its lunch hour arrival; it will return as Train 21 at 5:30PM. Photo by Robert P. Townley.

TWIN TERMINALS IN DENISON. Train 14 is wying into the TE Denison station; notice that the hostler has lowered the slider pole and is using the wheel pole for safer backing. Building in background is the Katy passenger station. Bob Townley took this photo in August 1948 when the Katy had its own passenger trains and competed for business with the TE, at least for through passengers.

EARLY AFTERNOON in the Waco Terminal. This 1942 scene shows 308, 317, 318. (TERA)

OFF-STREET LOADING AT CORSICANA. While they didn't roll out a red carpet for the passengers, this view shows that it at least had a cement walkway. The "Blue Bonnet" is about to sail for Dallas as Train 626 while car 312 in the rear (no, this isn't an MU train) has just arrived. Flight of birds over No. 316 is really the trolley wire with its pull-offs and insulator hardware. (I)

HERE IN THE WACO TERMINAL No. 328 has just unloaded its passengers from Dallas and there, almost within fenderbending range, is motor 314 (ex-313) ready to go north again. Photo by Robert P. Townley.

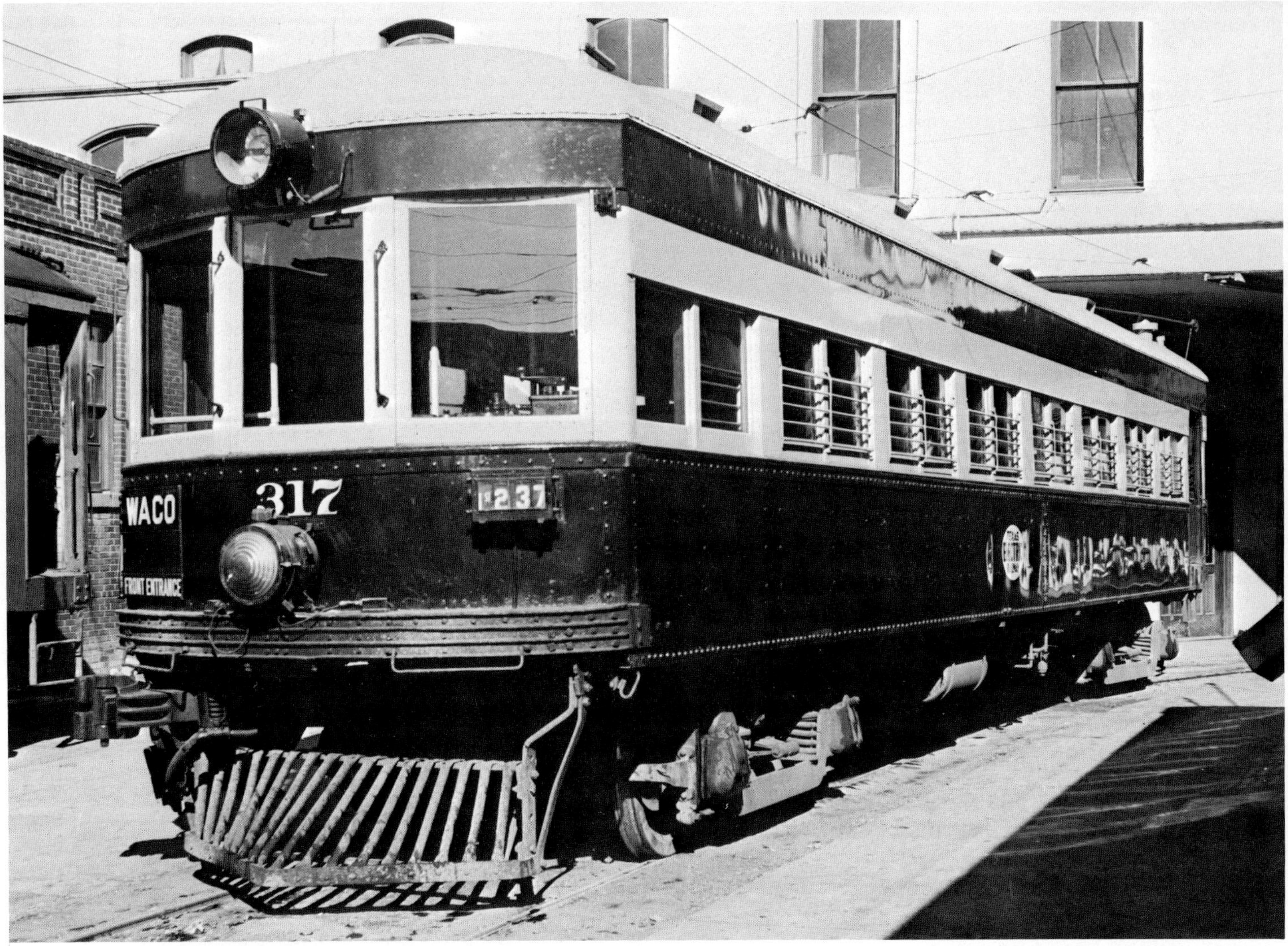

EARLY MORNING SHOT of second No. 317 (ex-first 311) which had laid overnight in the Waco terminal having arrived there at 12:25AM as Train 237. The tip of the pilot looks like car hit an oil slick somewhere. (TERA)

STUDY THE TRACK pattern and you will become convinced that this is none other than the Waco Terminal. Express trailer 620 having rolled into town behind a passenger motor on train 221 is now being hostled around the terminal yard and is about to be spotted alongside the express station for unloading. The wheel pole being used by the passenger coach is your clue to the backing movement that is taking place. (TERA)

Dallas was the hub

"BIG D" HAS ALWAYS THOUGHT BIG, and its centrally located interurban terminal was no exception to the pattern. It compared favorably in size and importance with those in such midwestern traction centers as Columbus, Dayton, Detroit—even Indianapolis. Here's an aerial view of the terminal loading area, circa early 1940s after TE became the sole rail tenant. Only one of the original seven tracks was missing by this time, used by the Fort Worth-Dallas buses as well as tracks 3 and 4. Wedge-shaped building at top was intended for off-duty trainmen as well as car cleaners. A passenger coach is the lone occupant of the storage tracks at top right; original plans called for tracks enough to store 18 cars on the lot. Now the rubber-tired enemy is occupying the biggest part of the storage area. Photo from M.D. McCarter.

HERE THE HOSTLERS in Dallas are shifting car 328 on the throat track which was located on the east side of the property. The operator's hand is visible in position on the controller; the man in the rear door looks like he is about to drop off of the car as soon as they clear the switch. These nifty lightweight cars were the favorites of crews and passengers alike. Photo by Robert P. Townley.

YES INDEED THERE WERE SERVICE PITS under at least one of the Dallas Interurban Terminal tracks. Photo at left by Walter P. Donalson Jr. shows car 363 in position for running maintenance while motor coach RPO No. 350 is being readied for the morning mail run to Denison. It's December 27, 1948—only three days until the end of all rail service. Photo at right shows the car cleaners at work in the terminal; three cars are being groomed for their next runs. (TERA)

THE DALLAS INTERURBAN TERMINAL could be a very busy place, especially back in the Roaring Twenties. The big Fort Worth car on the right has room on track 2, but the Trinity Heights Stone & Webster city car has him blocked. Track 4 looks like it has a three-car train, while track No. 6 sports one of the shorty parlor trailers. Some of the drivers of those automobiles parked in the foreground used to come to town by interurban though the TE brass didn't yet know how deadly a competition the flivver was destined to provide. How many of those autos on the parking lot can you identify? There are only three closed jobs in the whole row. A fine glass plate negative from Charles A. Smallwood.

TEXAS ELECTRIC CARRIED THE MAIL in arch-windowed style. This early morning shot catches RPO No. 362 being readied for its departure from the Dallas Interurban Terminal at 9:05AM as Train 10. Car 362 was once No. 12 and performed the regular mail runs along with its partner, the 360. (TERA)

THE OTHER RAILWAY POST OFFICE car, 360, performs fancy sideswing coming off Lane Street while crossing Jackson in order to get on to the throat track to the Dallas Interurban Terminal. Every arriving car had to do this ballet do-se-do to reach its assigned track. Photo from M.D. McCarter.

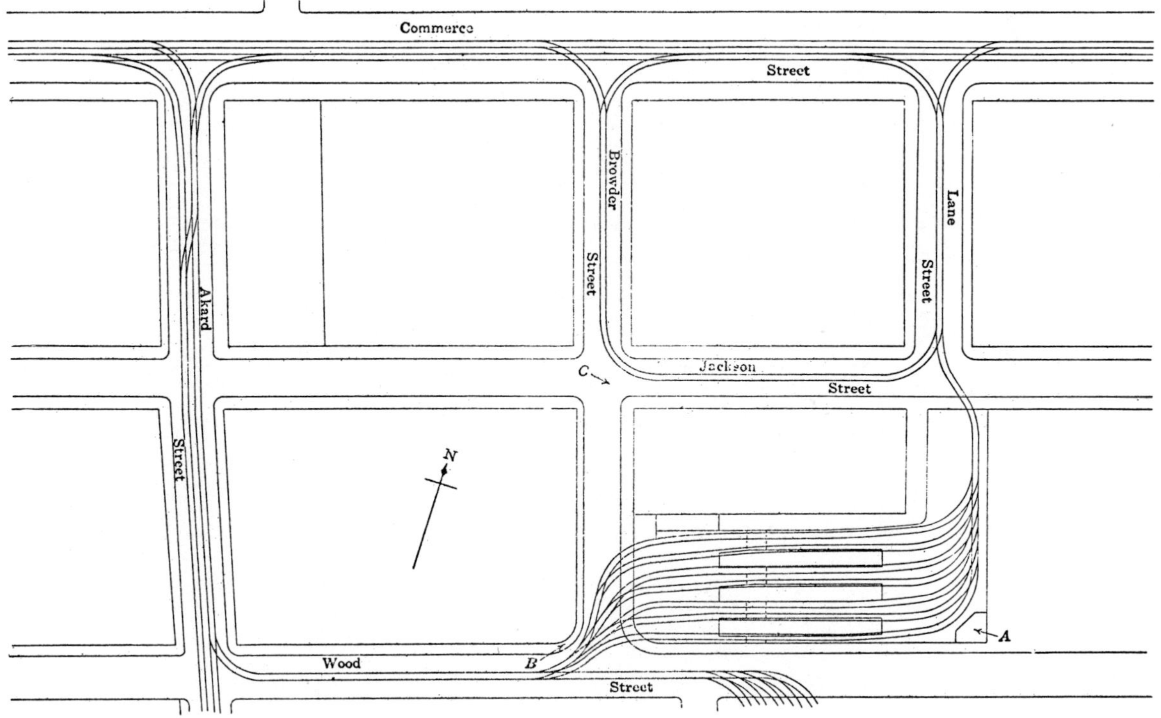

TRACK LAYOUT OF DALLAS INTERURBAN TERMINAL SHOWING CONNECTIONS WITH TRACKS ON ADJOINING STREETS

EVERY MAJOR ELECTRIC RAILWAY had a big shops complex and TE was no exception. We're looking at the south side of Monroe Shops. From left to right, we see: The sheet metal shop. The main bay or machine shop which has motors on all three tracks. A 15-ton box crane served this bay on rails 21 feet 8 inches apart. Carpenter and paint shops were in the next wing. Peaked roof building housed odds and ends. Next there were three long storage tracks with a coal storage bin at the end of the third track—and there were three short storage tracks and a railyard behind them. Photo from M.D. McCarter.

OLDER PHOTO taken inside Monroe Shops shows a lot of activity is taking place. The carpenters have been rebuilding a large car giving it a new end. Center track holds a freshly painted dark green car and on the right track sits one of the "banty's," three of which became parlor car trailers. This car is probably No. 103 but since it still has its trolley pole it isn't a trailer yet. C.V. Hess Collection.

TEXAS ELECTRIC's entrances into Dallas from both south and north are shown on 1925 map, in heavy lines. Going north out of the business district, cars for Denison and Sherman used the Dallas Railway & Terminal's Belmont line which included several miles of slow street running. The Waco and Corsicana lines to the south travelled the Trinity Heights local car line, mostly on private right-of-way. The interurbans were also speeded by the long and spectacular Trinity River viaduct used jointly by interurban and city cars. In later years, the Trinity Heights car line was taken over by the DR&T. Fort Worth, Terrell and Denton interurban lines, operated by other companies, also are indicated. (MS).

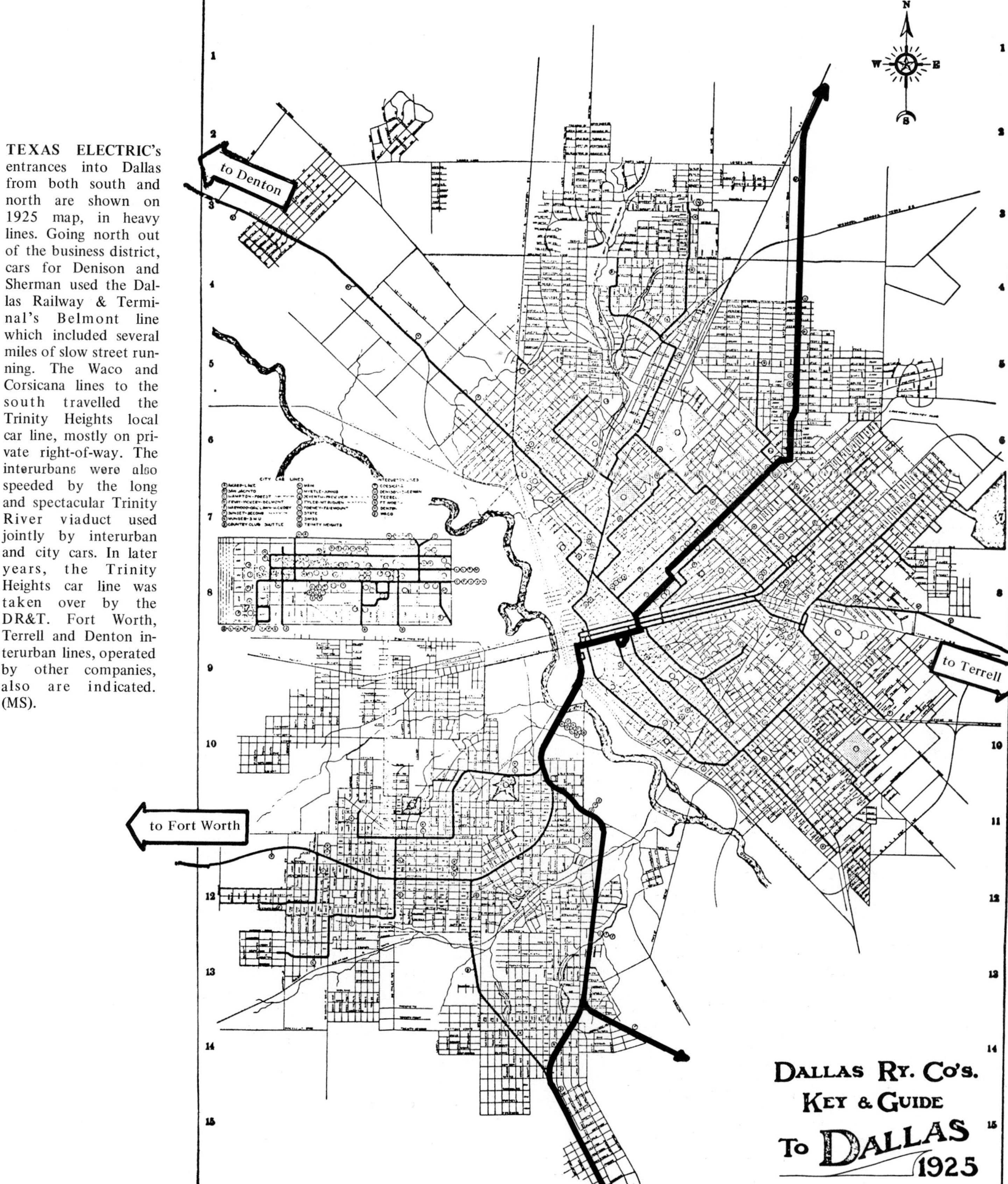

TEXAS ELECTRIC RAILWAY COMPANY

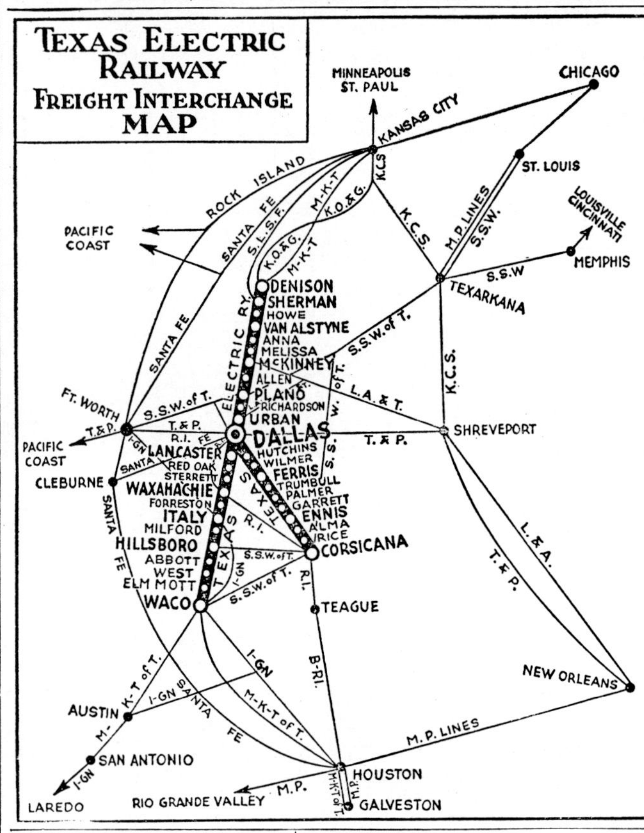

EXECUTIVE, OPERATING AND MECHANICAL DEPTS.
Interurban Building, Dallas, Tex.

JAS. P. GRIFFIN . . . . President
C. F. McAULIFF . . Vice-President and Purch. Agent
D. W. MILAM . . . . Auditor (Overcharge Claims)
H. G. FLOYD . . . . Superintendent
W. SILVUS . . . . Superintendent Motive Power

TRAFFIC AND CLAIM DEPARTMENTS
601 Young Street, Dallas, Tex.

A. E. MORRIS, Traffic Manager.
TOM GREEN, General Freight Agent, Waco, Tex.
F. D. WILKINS, General Claim Agent.
C. E. LENNON, Asst. General Freight and Pas. Agent.
H. C. McINTOSH, Asst. General Passenger Agent.
C. N. DUNCAN, General Agent.
W. J. GRISSETT, Division Freight and Passenger Agent, Waco, Tex.
M. T. DOOLING, General Agent, 344 Pierce Building, St. Louis, Mo.
J. P. PRESSLY, General Agent, 339 West Building, Houston, Tex.
E. C. GUION, General Agent, 324 Balter Building, New Orleans, La.
GEO. H. DIRMEYER, Commercial Agt., Sherman, Tex.
A. B. WILLIAMS, Commercial Agent, Corsicana, Tex.
E. R. BICK, General Agent, 309 South La Salle Street, Chicago, Ill.
E. E. HALE, General Agent, 306 South 4th Street, Louisville, Ky.
L. H. SCHREIBER, General Agent, 536 Ry. Exchange Bldg, Kansas City, Mo.
H. W. PATTERSON, General Agent, 291 Broadway, New York, N. Y.
J. J. ANGELL, General Agent, 601 Empire Building, Birmingham, Ala.

FREIGHT SERVICE

Fast dependable carload service from the North, East and Texas Gulf Ports. As intermediate or destination carrier.

Excellent package car service from Dallas to Austin, Houston, San Antonio, the Winter Garden and the Rio Grande Valley.

Twice-a-day merchandise service to all Texas Electric Railway points.

Free pickup and delivery service on all Texas less-car-load traffic.

DALLAS-DENISON DIVISION.

January, 1936.	Mls.	.....	.....	A M	A M	A M	A M	P M	P M	P M	P M	P M	P M	P M	P M	.....
Dallas ....lve.	0	.....	.....	*7 00	*8 00	*9 00	*11 00	*1 00	†2 00	*3 00	*4 00	*5 00	†6 00	*7 00	*9 00	.....
Plano	19.5	.....	A M	7 50	8 50	9 50	11 50	1 50	2 50	3 50	4 50	5 50	6 50	7 50	9 50	.....
McKinney	33.0	.....	†7 12	8 12	9 12	10 12	12 12	2 12	3 12	4 12	5 12	6 12	7 12	8 12	10 12	.....
Van Alstyne	49.8	A M	7 42	8 42	9 42	10 42	12 42	2 42	3 42	4 42	5 42	6 42	P M	8 42	10 42	.....
Sherman	66.2	*7 13	8 13	9 13	10 13	11 13	1 13	3 13	4 13	5 13	6 13	7 13	.....	9 13	11 13	.....
Denison ....arr.	76.5	7 40	8 40	9 40	10 40	11 40	1 40	3 40	4 40	5 40	6 40	7 40	.....	9 40	11 40	.....
STATIONS.	.....	A M	A M	A M	A M	Noon	P M	P M	P M	P M	P M	P M	P M	P M	.....	.....
Denison ....lve.	.....	*5 40	†7 00	*8 00	*10 00	*12 00	*2 00	*3 00	*4 00	*5 00	†6 00	*7 00	*9 00	*11 45	.....	.....
Sherman	.....	6 09	7 29	8 29	10 29	12 29	2 29	3 29	4 29	5 29	6 29	7 29	9 29	12 14	.....	.....
Van Alstyne	A M	6 40	8 00	9 00	11 00	1 00	3 00	4 00	5 00	6 00	7 00	8 00	10 00	A M	.....	.....
McKinney	†6 20	7 08	8 28	9 28	11 28	1 28	3 28	4 28	5 28	6 28	7 28	8 28	10 28	.....	.....	.....
Plano	6 43	7 30	8 50	9 50	11 50	1 50	3 50	4 50	5 50	6 50	P M	8 50	10 50	.....	.....	.....
Dallas ....arr.	7 38	8 25	9 40	10 40	12 40	2 40	4 40	5 40	6 40	7 40	.....	9 40	11 40	.....	.....	.....

DALLAS-WACO DIVISION.

January, 1936.	Mls.	.....	A M	A M	A M	A M	A M	P M	P M	P M	P M	P M	P M	P M	P M	P M
Dallas ....lve.	0	.....	*5 30	*7 30	*8 30	*9 30	*11 30	*1 30	*2 30	*3 30	*4 30	*5 30	†6 15	*7 30	*9 30	*11 05
Lancaster	15.1	.....	6 07	8 07	9 07	10 07	12 07	2 07	3 07	4 07	5 07	6 07	6 58	8 07	10 07	11 43
Waxahachie	30.7	.....	6 34	8 34	9 34	10 34	12 34	2 34	3 34	4 34	5 34	6 34	P M	8 34	10 34	12 10
Italy	45.1	A M	6 56	8 56	9 56	10 56	12 56	2 56	3 56	4 56	5 56	6 56	.....	8 56	10 56	A M
Hillsboro	64.2	†6 40	7 28	9 28	10 28	11 28	1 28	3 28	4 28	5 28	6 28	7 28	....	9 28	11 28	.....
West	79.6	7 06	7 53	9 53	10 53	11 53	1 53	3 53	4 53	5 53	6 53	7 53	.....	9 53	11 53	.....
Waco ....arr.	97.2	7 40	8 25	10 25	11 25	12 25	2 25	4 25	5 25	6 25	7 25	8 25	.....	10 25	12 25	.....
STATIONS.	.....	.....	A M	A M	A M	A M	A M	P M	P M	P M	P M	P M	P M	P M	P M	.....
Waco ....lve.	.....	.....	*5 20	*7 00	*8 00	*9 00	*11 00	*1 00	*2 00	*3 00	*4 00	*5 00	†6 00	*7 00	*9 00	.....
West	.....	.....	5 52	7 34	8 34	9 34	11 34	1 34	2 34	3 34	4 34	5 34	6 34	7 34	9 34	.....
Hillsboro	.....	.....	6 15	7 58	8 58	9 58	11 58	1 58	2 58	3 58	4 58	5 58	6 58	7 58	9 58	.....
Italy	.....	A M	6 44	8 27	9 27	10 27	12 27	2 27	3 27	4 27	5 27	6 27	P M	8 27	10 27	.....
Waxahachie	A M	*6 35	7 09	8 51	9 51	10 51	12 51	2 51	3 51	4 51	5 51	6 51	.....	8 51	10 51	.....
Lancaster	†6 18	7 02	7 36	9 18	10 18	11 18	1 18	3 18	4 18	5 18	6 18	7 18	.....	9 18	11 18	.....
Dallas ....arr.	6 55	7 40	8 15	9 55	10 55	11 55	1 55	3 55	4 55	5 55	6 55	7 55	.....	9 55	11 55	.....

DALLAS-CORSICANA DIVISION.

January, 1936.	Ms.	A M	A M	A M	A M	P M	P M	P M	P M	P M	P M	P M	P M
Dallas ......lve.	0	†6 00	*7 40	*8 40	*10 40	*12 40	*2 40	*4 40	*5 40	†6 15	*7 40	*9 40	*11 00
Ferris	20.8	6 41	8 25	9 25	11 25	1 25	3 25	5 25	6 25	7 01	8 25	10 25	11 45
Ennis	35.6	7 10	8 51	9 51	11 51	1 51	3 51	5 51	6 51	P M	8 51	10 51	12 11
Corsicana ..arr.	56.3	7 49	9 30	10 30	12 30	2 30	4 30	6 30	7 30	.....	9 30	11 30	12 50
STATIONS.	....	A M	A M	A M	A M	A M	P M	P M	P M	P M	P M	P M	.....
Corsicana ..lve.	....	†6 00	*6 40	*7 40	*9 40	*11 40	*1 40	*2 40	*3 40	*5 40	*7 40	*9 40	.....
Ennis	A M	6 35	7 15	8 15	10 15	12 15	2 15	3 15	4 15	6 15	8 15	10 15	.....
Ferris	†6 35	7 01	7 41	8 41	10 41	12 41	2 41	3 41	4 41	6 41	8 41	10 41	.....
Dallas ....arr.	7 25	7 50	8 30	9 30	11 30	1 30	3 30	4 30	5 30	7 30	9 30	11 30	.....

ALL TRAINS CARRY BAGGAGE AND PREFERRED EXPRESS.

EXPLANATION OF SIGNS.

* Daily.
† Daily, except Sunday.
STANDARD—*Central time.*

It was 'the Electric Way'

THE TEXAS ELECTRIC WAS big-time electric railroading at its best, and don't you forget it! Take the famous Waxahachie trestle, for instance. This was a long 800-foot, 40-foot-high spanner that leaped over both the Missouri-Kansas-Texas and the Burlington/Rock Island railroads on the south edge of Waxahachie. The engineers who laid out the TE spared no expense to give Texans an interurban they could brag about. Photo from M.D. McCarter.

REPRINT

TEXAS ELECTRIC RAILWAY COMPANY

PACKAGE CAR SERVICE

Merchandise or less-car-load shipments handled on "Baggage and Express Trains".

PREFERRED SERVICE

will be handled on all passenge cars, when space in cars and nature of merchandise permits, when delivered to our stations, for which there is a small additional charge.

ROUTE "ELECTRIC EXPRESS"

Free Store Door Delivery at Destination

C. O. D. Collections Promptly Returned

CALL US FOR CAR-LOAD RATES via TEXAS ELECTRIC RAILWAY

Bus Connections

Direct connections at Dallas with bus lines to all points in the United States.

Direct connections at Waco and Corsicana with bus lines to all points East, South and West.

Direct connections at Sherman and Denison with bus lines to all points North, East and West.

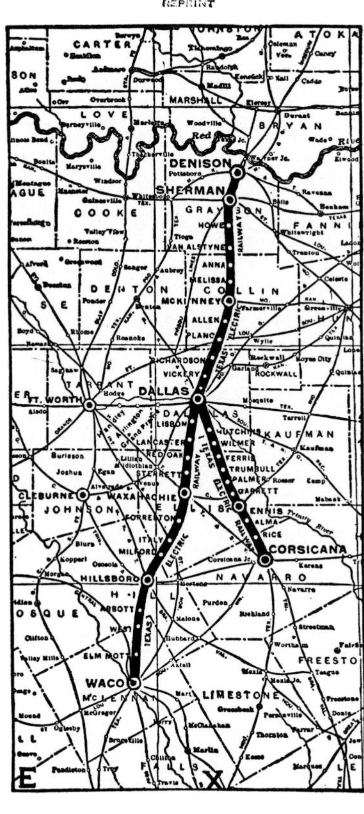

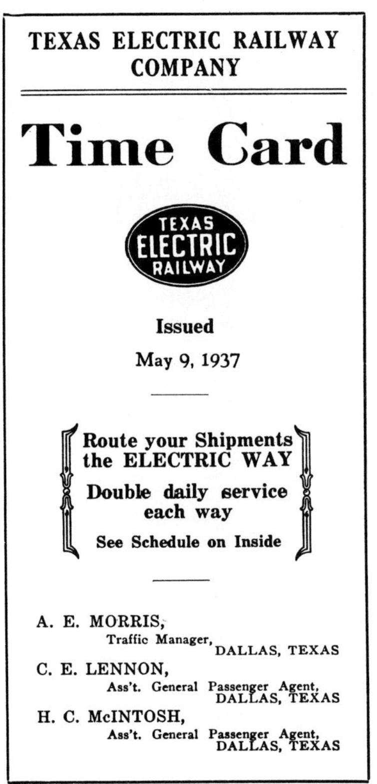

TEXAS ELECTRIC RAILWAY COMPANY

Time Card

TEXAS ELECTRIC RAILWAY

Issued

May 9, 1937

Route your Shipments the ELECTRIC WAY

Double daily service each way

See Schedule on Inside

A. E. MORRIS,
Traffic Manager, DALLAS, TEXAS

C. E. LENNON,
Ass't. General Passenger Agent, DALLAS, TEXAS

H. C. McINTOSH,
Ass't. General Passenger Agent, DALLAS, TEXAS

ON THE NEXT THREE PAGES we reproduce Texas Electric public timetables representative of two latter-day eras: before and after the abandonment of the Corsicana division. (TERA)

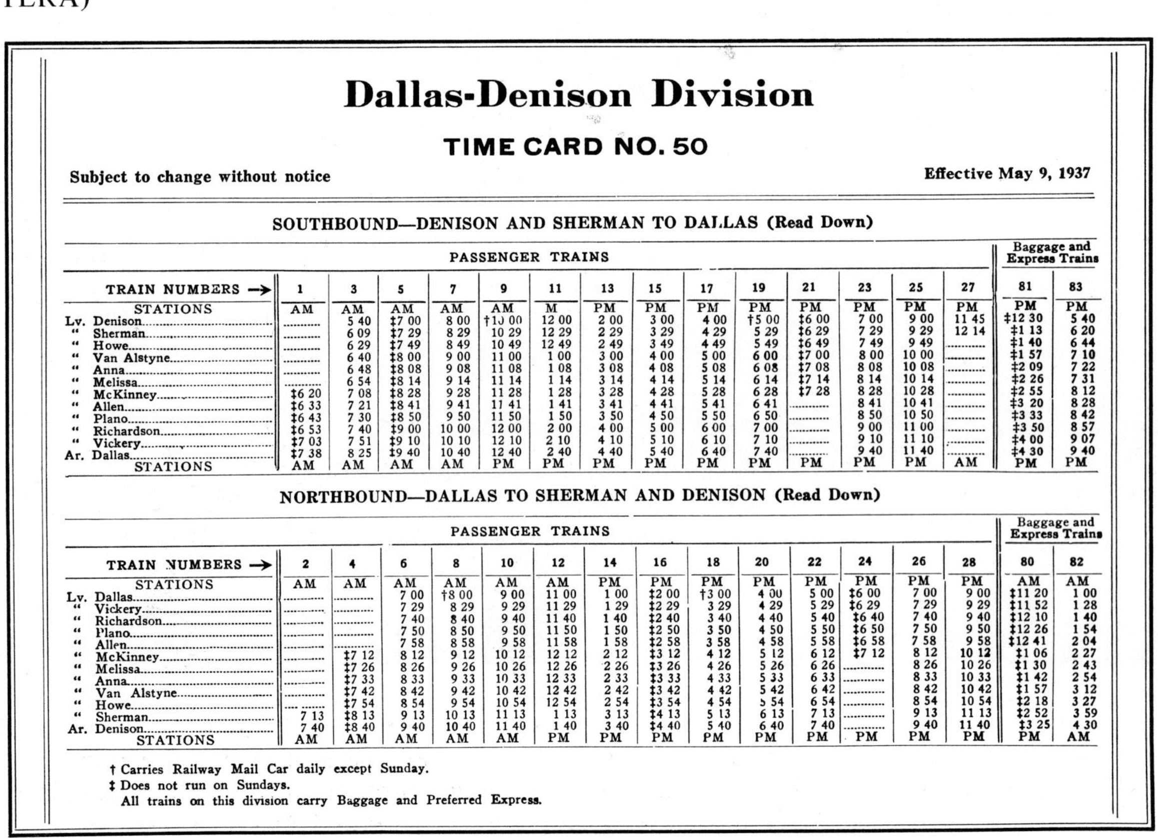

Dallas-Denison Division

TIME CARD NO. 50

Subject to change without notice — **Effective May 9, 1937**

SOUTHBOUND—DENISON AND SHERMAN TO DALLAS (Read Down)

	PASSENGER TRAINS														Baggage and Express Trains	
TRAIN NUMBERS →	1	3	5	7	9	11	13	15	17	19	21	23	25	27	81	83
STATIONS	AM	AM	AM	AM	AM	M	PM	PM	PM	PM	PM	PM	PM	PM	PM	PM
Lv. Denison	....	5 40	‡7 00	8 00	†10 00	12 00	2 00	3 00	4 00	†5 00	‡6 00	7 00	9 00	11 45	‡12 30	5 40
" Sherman	....	6 09	‡7 29	8 29	10 29	12 29	2 29	3 29	4 29	5 29	‡6 29	7 29	9 29	12 14	‡1 13	6 20
" Howe	....	6 29	‡7 49	8 49	10 49	12 49	2 49	3 49	4 49	5 49	‡6 49	7 49	9 49	....	‡1 40	6 44
" Van Alstyne	....	6 40	‡8 00	9 00	11 00	1 00	3 00	4 00	5 00	6 00	‡7 00	8 00	10 00	....	‡1 57	7 10
" Anna	....	6 48	‡8 08	9 08	11 08	1 08	3 08	4 08	5 08	6 08	‡7 08	8 08	10 08	....	‡2 09	7 22
" Melissa	....	6 54	‡8 14	9 14	11 14	1 14	3 14	4 14	5 14	6 14	‡7 14	8 14	10 14	....	‡2 26	7 31
" McKinney	‡6 20	7 08	‡8 28	9 28	11 28	1 28	3 28	4 28	5 28	6 28	‡7 28	8 28	10 28	....	‡2 55	8 12
" Allen	‡6 33	7 21	‡8 41	9 41	11 41	1 41	3 41	4 41	5 41	6 41	....	8 41	10 41	....	‡3 20	8 28
" Plano	‡6 43	7 30	‡8 50	9 50	11 50	1 50	3 50	4 50	5 50	6 50	....	8 50	10 50	....	‡3 33	8 42
" Richardson	‡6 53	7 40	‡9 00	10 00	12 00	2 00	4 00	5 00	6 00	7 00	....	9 00	11 00	....	‡3 50	8 57
" Vickery	‡7 03	7 51	‡9 10	10 10	12 10	2 10	4 10	5 10	6 10	7 10	....	9 10	11 10	....	‡4 00	9 07
Ar. Dallas	‡7 38	8 25	‡9 40	10 40	12 40	2 40	4 40	5 40	6 40	7 40	....	9 40	11 40	....	‡4 30	9 40
STATIONS	AM	AM	AM	AM	PM	PM	PM	PM	PM	PM	PM	PM	PM	AM	PM	PM

NORTHBOUND—DALLAS TO SHERMAN AND DENISON (Read Down)

	PASSENGER TRAINS														Baggage and Express Trains	
TRAIN NUMBERS →	2	4	6	8	10	12	14	16	18	20	22	24	26	28	80	82
STATIONS	AM	AM	AM	AM	AM	AM	PM	PM	PM	PM	PM	PM	PM	PM	AM	AM
Lv. Dallas	....	....	7 00	†8 00	9 00	11 00	1 00	‡2 00	†3 00	4 00	5 00	‡6 00	7 00	9 00	‡11 20	1 00
" Vickery	....	....	7 29	8 29	9 29	11 29	1 29	‡2 29	3 29	4 29	5 29	‡6 29	7 29	9 29	‡11 52	1 28
" Richardson	....	....	7 40	8 40	9 40	11 40	1 40	‡2 40	3 40	4 40	5 40	‡6 40	7 40	9 40	‡12 10	1 40
" Plano	....	....	7 50	8 50	9 50	11 50	1 50	‡2 50	3 50	4 50	5 50	‡6 50	7 50	9 50	‡12 26	1 54
" Allen	....	....	7 58	8 58	9 58	11 58	1 58	‡2 58	3 58	4 58	5 58	‡6 58	7 58	9 58	‡12 41	2 04
" McKinney	....	‡7 12	8 12	9 12	10 12	12 12	2 12	‡3 12	4 12	5 12	6 12	‡7 12	8 12	10 12	‡1 06	2 27
" Melissa	....	‡7 26	8 26	9 26	10 26	12 26	2 26	‡3 26	4 26	5 26	6 26	....	8 26	10 26	‡1 30	2 43
" Anna	....	‡7 33	8 33	9 33	10 33	12 33	2 33	‡3 33	4 33	5 33	6 33	....	8 33	10 33	‡1 42	2 54
" Van Alstyne	....	‡7 42	8 42	9 42	10 42	12 42	2 42	‡3 42	4 42	5 42	6 42	....	8 42	10 42	‡1 57	3 12
" Howe	....	‡7 54	8 54	9 54	10 54	12 54	2 54	‡3 54	4 54	5 54	6 54	....	8 54	10 54	‡2 18	3 27
" Sherman	7 13	‡8 13	9 13	10 13	11 13	1 13	3 13	‡4 13	5 13	6 13	7 13	....	9 13	11 13	‡2 52	3 59
Ar. Denison	7 40	‡8 40	9 40	10 40	11 40	1 40	3 40	‡4 40	5 40	6 40	7 40	....	9 40	11 40	‡3 25	4 30
STATIONS	AM	AM	AM	AM	AM	PM	PM	PM	PM	PM	PM	PM	PM	PM	PM	AM

† Carries Railway Mail Car daily except Sunday.
‡ Does not run on Sundays.
All trains on this division carry Baggage and Preferred Express.

Dallas-Waco Division

Subject to change without notice — **TIME CARD NO. 113** — **Effective April 17, 1932**

SOUTHBOUND—DALLAS TO WACO (Read Down)

TRAIN NUMBERS →	211	213	215	217	219	221	223	225	227	229	231	233	235	237	239	511	
	PASSENGER TRAINS															Baggage and Express Trains	
STATIONS	AM	AM	AM	AM	AM	AM	PM	PM	PM	PM	PM	PM	PM	PM	PM	AM	AM
Lv. Dallas	....	5 30	7 30	8 30	9 30	11 30	1 30	2 30	3 30	4 30	5 30	‡6 15	7 30	9 30	11 05	12 15	§11 30
" Oak Cliff Junction	....	5 40	7 40	8 40	9 40	11 40	1 40	2 40	3 40	4 40	5 40	‡6 25	7 40	9 40	11 15	12 20	§11 40
" Monroe	....	5 49	7 49	8 49	9 49	11 49	1 49	2 49	3 49	4 49	5 49	‡6 34	7 49	9 49	11 24	12 27	§11 49
" Lisbon	....	5 54	7 54	8 54	9 54	11 54	1 54	2 54	3 54	4 54	5 54	‡6 39	7 54	9 54	11 30	12 32	§11 54
" Lancaster	....	6 07	8 07	9 07	10 07	12 07	2 07	3 07	4 07	5 07	6 07	‡6 58	8 07	10 07	11 43	12 48	§12 07
" Red Oak	....	6 17	8 17	9 17	10 17	12 17	2 17	3 17	4 17	5 17	6 17	....	8 17	10 17	11 53	1 00	§12 17
" Sterrett	....	6 22	8 22	9 22	10 22	12 22	2 22	3 22	4 22	5 22	6 22	....	8 22	10 22	11 58	1 05	§12 22
" Waxahachie	....	6 34	8 34	9 34	10 34	12 34	2 34	3 34	4 34	5 34	6 34	....	8 34	10 34	12 10	1 25	§12 34
" Forreston	....	6 48	8 48	9 48	10 48	12 48	2 48	3 48	4 48	5 48	6 48	....	8 48	10 48	....	1 42	§12 48
" Italy	....	6 56	8 56	9 56	10 56	12 56	2 56	3 56	4 56	5 56	6 56	....	8 56	10 56	....	2 07	§12 56
" Milford	....	7 06	9 06	10 06	11 06	1 06	3 06	4 06	5 06	6 06	7 06	....	9 06	11 06	....	2 25	§1 06
" Hillsboro	‡6 40	7 28	9 28	10 28	11 28	1 28	3 28	4 28	5 28	6 28	7 28	....	9 28	11 28	....	3 03	§1 28
" Abbott	‡6 56	7 44	9 44	10 44	11-44	1 44	3 44	4 44	5 44	6 44	7 44	....	9 44	11 44	....	3 25	§1 44
" West	‡7 06	7 53	9 53	10 53	11 53	1 53	3 53	4 53	5 53	6 53	7 53	....	9 53	11 53	....	3 40	§1 53
" Elm Mott	‡7 21	8 05	10 05	11 05	12 05	2 05	4 05	5 05	6 05	7 05	8 05	....	10 05	12 05	....	3 55	§2 05
Ar. Waco	‡7 40	8 25	10 25	11 25	12 25	2 25	4 25	5 25	6 25	7 25	8 25	....	10 25	12 25	....	4 15	§2 25
STATIONS	AM	AM	AM	AM	PM	PM	PM	PM	PM	PM	PM	PM	PM	AM	AM	AM	PM

NORTHBOUND—WACO TO DALLAS (Read Down)

TRAIN NUMBERS →	210	212	214	216	218	220	222	224	226	228	230	232	234	236	238	512	514
	PASSENGER TRAINS															Baggage and Express Trains	
STATIONS	AM	AM	AM	AM	AM	AM	AM	PM	PM	PM	PM	PM	PM	PM	PM	AM	PM
Lv. Waco	....	....	5 20	7 00	8 00	9 00	11 00	1 00	2 00	3 00	4 00	5 00	‡6 00	7 00	9 00	‡10 10	6 30
" Elm Mott	....	....	5 40	7 21	8 21	9 21	11 21	1 21	2 21	3 21	4 21	5 21	‡6 21	7 21	9 21	‡10 30	6 50
" West	....	....	5 52	7 34	8 34	9 34	11 34	1 34	2 34	3 34	4 34	5 34	‡6 34	7 34	9 34	‡10 53	7 14
" Abbott	....	....	6 02	7 44	8 44	9 44	11 44	1 44	2 44	3 44	4 44	5 44	‡6 44	7 44	9 44	‡11 02	7 27
" Hillsboro	....	....	6 15	7 58	8 58	9 58	11 58	1 58	2 58	3 58	4 58	5 58	‡6 58	7 58	9 58	‡11 28	8 03
" Milford	....	....	6 34	8 17	9 17	10 17	12 17	2 17	3 17	4 17	5 17	6 17	....	8 17	10 17	‡11 53	8 30
" Italy	....	....	6 44	8 27	9 27	10 27	12 27	2 27	3 27	4 27	5 27	6 27	....	8 27	10 27	‡12 33	8 56
" Forreston	....	....	6 53	8 35	9 35	10 35	12 35	2 35	3 35	4 35	5 35	6 35	....	8 35	10 35	‡12 48	9 05
" Waxahachie	....	6 35	7 09	8 51	9 51	10 51	12 51	2 51	3 51	4 51	5 51	6 51	....	8 51	10 51	‡1 15	9 33
" Sterrett	....	6 45	7 19	9 01	10 01	11 01	1 01	3 01	4 01	5 01	6 01	7 01	....	9 01	11 01	‡1 27	9 44
" Red Oak	....	6 50	7 24	9 06	10 06	11 06	1 06	3 06	4 06	5 06	6 06	7 06	....	9 06	11 06	‡1 33	9 50
" Lancaster	‡6 18	7 02	7 36	9 18	10 18	11 18	1 18	3 18	4 18	5 18	6 18	7 18	....	9 18	11 18	‡1 47	10 07
" Lisbon	‡6 30	7 14	7 48	9 30	10 30	11 30	1 30	3 30	4 30	5 30	6 30	7 30	....	9 30	11 30	‡2 04	10 21
" Monroe	‡6 35	7 21	7 54	9 35	10 35	11 35	1 35	3 35	4 35	5 35	6 35	7 35	....	9 35	11 35	‡2 09	10 26
" Oak Cliff Junction	‡6 42	7 27	8 01	9 42	10 42	11 42	1 42	3 42	4 42	5 42	6 42	7 42	....	9 42	11 42	‡2 14	10 31
Ar. Dallas	‡6 55	7 40	8 15	9 55	10 55	11 55	1 55	3 55	4 55	5 55	6 55	7 55	....	9 55	11 55	‡2 28	10 45
STATIONS	AM	AM	AM	AM	AM	AM	PM	PM	PM	PM	PM	PM	PM	PM	PM	PM	PM

‡ Does not run on Sundays.
§ Express trailer operated on regular 11:30 A. M. Passenger Car daily, except Sunday.
All trains on this division carry Baggage and Preferred Express.

WHILE THE DALLAS-DENISON table had been revised on May 9, 1937 (see preceding page) these two tables had been in effect for several years without change. (TERA)

Dallas-Corsicana Division

TIME CARD NO. 118

Subject to change without notice — **Effective June 17, 1934**

SOUTHBOUND—DALLAS TO CORSICANA (Read Down)

TRAIN NUMBERS →	615	617	619	621	623	625	627	629	631	633	635	637	701	
	PASSENGER TRAINS												Baggage and Express Trains	
STATIONS	AM	AM	AM	AM	PM	PM	PM	PM	PM	PM	PM	PM	AM	PM
Lv. Dallas	‡6 00	7 40	8 40	10 40	12 40	2 40	4 40	5 40	‡6 15	7 40	9 40	11 00	1 40	§12 40
" Oak Cliff Junction	‡6 10	7 50	8 50	10 50	12 50	2 50	4 50	5 50	‡6 25	7 50	9 50	11 10	1 47	§12 50
" Monroe	‡6 17	7 59	8 59	10 59	12 59	2 59	4 59	5 59	‡6 34	7 59	9 59	11 19	1 55	§12 59
" Hutchins	‡6 27	8 10	9 10	11 10	1 10	3 10	5 10	6 10	‡6 45	8 10	10 10	11 30	2 07	§1 10
" Wilmer	‡6 33	8 17	9 17	11 17	1 17	3 17	5 17	6 17	‡6 53	8 17	10 17	11 37	2 15	§1 17
" Ferris	‡6 41	8 25	9 25	11 25	1 25	3 25	5 25	6 25	‡7 01	8 25	10 25	11 45	2 37	§1 25
" Trumbull	‡6 48	8 30	9 30	11 30	1 30	3 30	5 30	6 30	....	8 30	10 30	11 50	2 43	§1 30
" Palmer	‡6 56	8 37	9 37	11 37	1 37	3 37	5 37	6 37	....	8 37	10 37	11 57	3 05	§1 37
" Garrett	‡7 02	8 43	9 43	11 43	1 43	3 43	5 43	6 43	....	8 43	10 43	12 03	3 11	§1 43
" Ennis	‡7 10	8 51	9 51	11 51	1 51	3 51	5 51	6 51	....	8 51	10 51	12 11	3 27	§1 51
" Alma	‡7 20	9 01	10 01	12 01	2 01	4 01	6 01	7 01	....	9 01	11 01	12 21	3 36	§2 01
" Rice	‡7 25	9 06	10 06	12 06	2 06	4 06	6 06	7 06	....	9 06	11 06	12 26	3 52	§2 06
Ar. Corsicana	‡7 49	9 30	10 30	12 30	2 30	4 30	6 30	7 30	....	9 30	11 30	12 50	4 15	§2 30
STATIONS	AM	AM	AM	PM	PM	PM	PM	PM	PM	PM	PM	AM	AM	PM

NORTHBOUND—CORSICANA TO DALLAS (Read Down)

TRAIN NUMBERS →	612	614	616	618	620	622	624	626	628	630	632	634	702
	PASSENGER TRAINS												Baggage and Express Train
STATIONS	AM	AM	AM	AM	AM	AM	PM	PM	PM	PM	PM	PM	PM
Lv. Corsicana	....	‡6 00	6 40	7 40	9 40	11 40	1 40	2 40	3 40	5 40	7 40	9 40	6 30
" Rice	....	‡6 19	6 59	7 59	9 59	11 59	1 59	2 59	3 59	5 59	7 59	9 59	6 54
" Alma	....	‡6 25	7 05	8 05	10 05	12 05	2 05	3 05	4 05	6 05	8 05	10 05	7 08
" Ennis	....	‡6 35	7 15	8 15	10 15	12 15	2 15	3 15	4 15	6 15	8 15	10 15	7 25
" Garrett	....	‡6 44	7 24	8 24	10 24	12 24	2 24	3 24	4 24	6 24	8 24	10 24	7 34
" Palmer	....	‡6 50	7 30	8 30	10 30	12 30	2 30	3 30	4 30	6 30	8 30	10 30	7 50
" Trumbull	....	‡6 56	7 36	8 36	10 36	12 36	2 36	3 36	4 36	6 36	8 36	10 36	7 56
" Ferris	‡6 35	‡7 01	7 41	8 41	10 41	12 41	2 41	3 41	4 41	6 41	8 41	10 41	8 05
" Wilmer	‡6 41	‡7 08	7 48	8 48	10 48	12 48	2 48	3 48	4 48	6 48	8 48	10 48	8 17
" Hutchins	‡6 49	‡7 15	7 55	8 55	10 55	12 55	2 55	3 55	4 55	6 55	8 55	10 55	8 24
" Monroe	‡7 03	‡7 27	8 07	9 07	11 07	1 07	3 07	4 07	5 07	7 07	9 07	11 07	8 36
" Oak Cliff Junction	‡7 10	‡7 35	8 15	9 15	11 15	1 15	3 15	4 15	5 15	7 15	9 15	11 15	8 45
Ar. Dallas	‡7 25	‡7 50	8 30	9 30	11 30	1 30	3 30	4 30	5 30	7 30	9 30	11 30	8 55
STATIONS	AM	AM	AM	AM	AM	PM	PM	PM	PM	PM	PM	PM	PM

‡ Does not run on Sundays.
§Express trailer operated on regular 12:40 P. M. Passenger Car daily, except Sunday.
All trains on this division carry Baggage and Preferred Express.

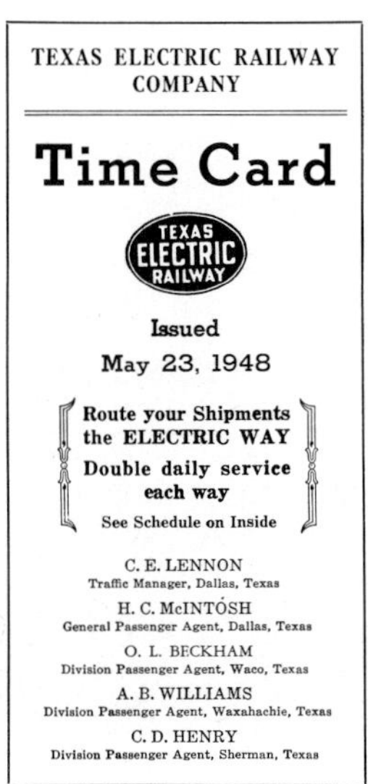

TEXAS ELECTRIC RAILWAY COMPANY

Time Card

Issued
May 23, 1948

Route your Shipments the ELECTRIC WAY
Double daily service each way
See Schedule on Inside

C. E. LENNON
Traffic Manager, Dallas, Texas

H. C. McINTOSH
General Passenger Agent, Dallas, Texas

O. L. BECKHAM
Division Passenger Agent, Waco, Texas

A. B. WILLIAMS
Division Passenger Agent, Waxahachie, Texas

C. D. HENRY
Division Passenger Agent, Sherman, Texas

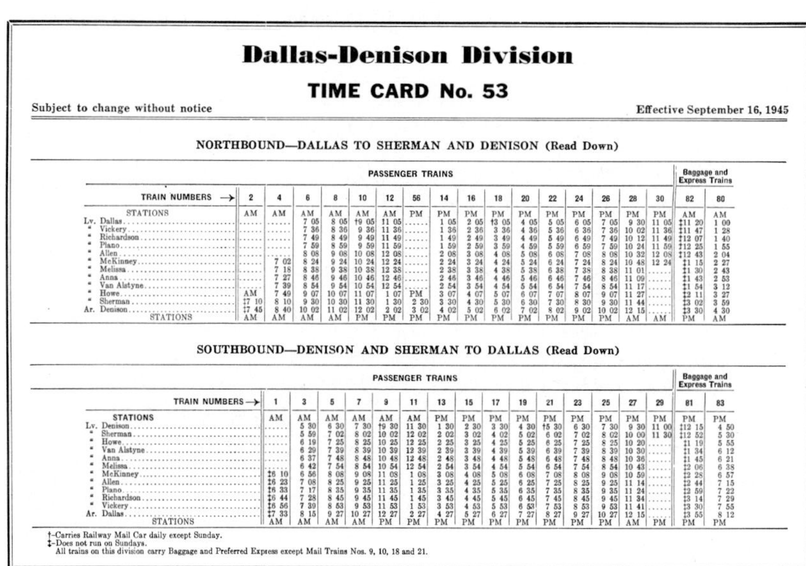

Dallas-Denison Division

TIME CARD No. 53

Subject to change without notice — Effective September 16, 1945

NORTHBOUND—DALLAS TO SHERMAN AND DENISON (Read Down)

	PASSENGER TRAINS																Baggage and Express Trains	
TRAIN NUMBERS →	2	4	6	8	10	12	56	14	16	18	20	22	24	26	28	30	82	80
STATIONS	AM	AM	AM	AM	AM	AM	PM	PM	PM	PM	PM	PM	PM	PM	PM	PM	AM	AM
Lv. Dallas	......	......	7 05	8 05	†9 05	11 05	......	1 05	2 05	†3 05	4 05	5 05	6 05	7 05	9 30	11 05	‡11 20	1 00
" Vickery	......	......	7 36	8 36	9 36	11 36	......	1 36	2 36	3 36	4 36	5 36	6 36	7 36	10 02	11 36	‡11 47	1 28
" Richardson	......	......	7 49	8 49	9 49	11 49	......	1 49	2 49	3 49	4 49	5 49	6 49	7 49	10 12	11 49	‡12 07	1 40
" Plano	......	......	7 59	8 59	9 59	11 59	......	1 59	2 59	3 59	4 59	5 59	6 59	7 59	10 24	11 59	‡12 25	1 55
" Allen	......	......	8 08	9 08	10 08	12 08	......	2 08	3 08	4 08	5 08	6 08	7 08	8 08	10 32	12 08	‡12 43	2 04
" McKinney	......	7 02	8 24	9 24	10 24	12 24	......	2 24	3 24	4 24	5 24	6 24	7 24	8 24	10 48	12 24	‡1 15	2 27
" Melissa	......	7 18	8 38	9 38	10 38	12 38	......	2 38	3 38	4 38	5 38	6 38	7 38	8 38	11 01	......	‡1 30	2 43
" Anna	......	7 27	8 46	9 46	10 46	12 46	......	2 46	3 46	4 46	5 46	6 46	7 46	8 46	11 09	......	‡1 43	2 53
" Van Alstyne	......	7 39	8 54	9 54	10 54	12 54	......	2 54	3 54	4 54	5 54	6 54	7 54	8 54	11 17	......	‡1 54	3 12
" Howe	AM	7 49	9 07	10 07	11 07	1 07	PM	3 07	4 07	5 07	6 07	7 07	8 07	9 07	11 27	......	‡2 11	3 27
" Sherman	‡7 10	8 10	9 30	10 30	11 30	1 30	2 30	3 30	4 30	5 30	6 30	7 30	8 30	9 30	11 44	......	‡3 02	3 59
Ar. Denison	‡7 45	8 40	10 02	11 02	12 02	2 02	3 02	4 02	5 02	6 02	7 02	8 02	9 02	10 02	12 15	......	‡3 30	4 30
STATIONS	AM	AM	AM	AM	PM	PM	PM	PM	PM	PM	PM	PM	PM	PM	AM	AM	PM	AM

SOUTHBOUND—DENISON AND SHERMAN TO DALLAS (Read Down)

	PASSENGER TRAINS															Baggage and Express Trains	
TRAIN NUMBERS →	1	3	5	7	9	11	13	15	17	19	21	23	25	27	29	81	83
STATIONS	AM	AM	AM	AM	AM	AM	PM	PM	PM	PM	PM	PM	PM	PM	PM	PM	PM
Lv. Denison	......	5 30	6 30	7 30	†9 30	11 30	1 30	2 30	3 30	4 30	†5 30	6 30	7 30	9 30	11 00	‡12 15	4 50
" Sherman	......	5 59	7 02	8 02	10 02	12 02	2 02	3 02	4 02	5 02	6 02	7 02	8 02	10 00	11 30	‡12 52	5 30
" Howe	......	6 19	7 25	8 25	10 25	12 25	2 25	3 25	4 25	5 25	6 25	7 25	8 25	10 20	......	‡1 19	5 55
" Van Alstyne	......	6 29	7 39	8 39	10 39	12 39	2 39	3 39	4 39	5 39	6 39	7 39	8 39	10 30	......	‡1 34	6 12
" Anna	......	6 37	7 48	8 48	10 48	12 48	2 48	3 48	4 48	5 48	6 48	7 48	8 48	10 36	......	‡1 45	6 21
" Melissa	......	6 42	7 54	8 54	10 54	12 54	2 54	3 54	4 54	5 54	6 54	7 54	8 54	10 43	......	‡2 06	6 38
" McKinney	‡6 10	6 56	8 08	9 08	11 08	1 08	3 08	4 08	5 08	6 08	7 08	8 08	9 08	10 59	......	‡2 28	6 57
" Allen	‡6 23	7 08	8 25	9 25	11 25	1 25	3 25	4 25	5 25	6 25	7 25	8 25	9 25	11 14	......	‡2 44	7 15
" Plano	‡6 33	7 17	8 35	9 35	11 35	1 35	3 35	4 35	5 35	6 35	7 35	8 35	9 35	11 24	......	‡2 59	7 22
" Richardson	‡6 44	7 28	8 45	9 45	11 45	1 45	3 45	4 45	5 45	6 45	7 45	8 45	9 45	11 34	......	‡3 14	7 29
" Vickery	‡6 56	7 30	8 53	9 53	11 53	1 53	3 53	4 53	5 53	6 53	7 53	8 53	9 53	11 41	......	‡3 30	7 55
Ar. Dallas	‡7 33	8 15	9 27	10 27	12 27	2 27	4 27	5 27	6 27	7 27	8 27	9 27	10 27	12 15	......	‡3 55	8 12
STATIONS	AM	AM	AM	AM	PM	PM	PM	PM	PM	PM	PM	PM	PM	AM	PM	PM	PM

†-Carries Railway Mail Car daily except Sunday.
‡-Does not run on Sundays.
All trains on this division carry Baggage and Preferred Express except Mail Trains Nos. 9, 10, 18 and 21.

THIS IS PROBABLY THE TEXAS ELECTRIC's last public timetable, still showing a very comprehensive schedule both north and south. The Corsicana branch is gone, but mainline service is little changed from a decade previous. They had even added a 2:30PM local from Sherman to Denison! (TERA)

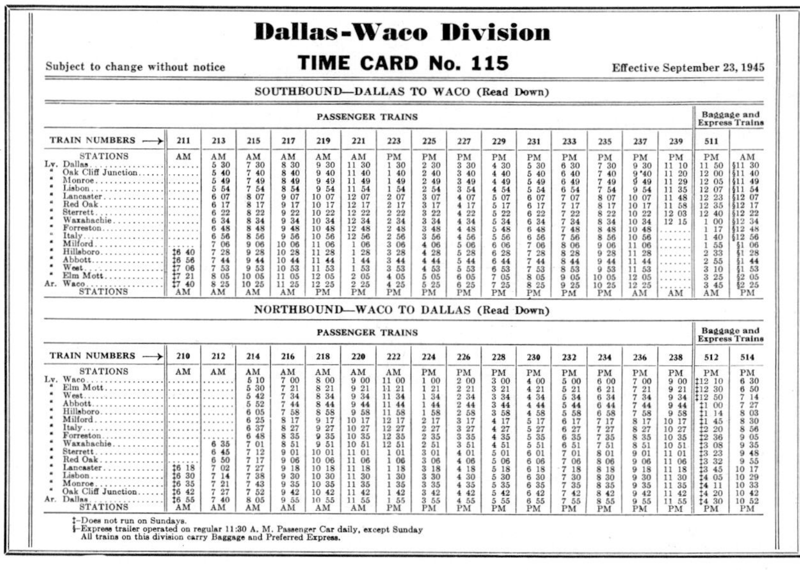

Dallas-Waco Division

TIME CARD No. 115

Subject to change without notice — Effective September 23, 1945

SOUTHBOUND—DALLAS TO WACO (Read Down)

	PASSENGER TRAINS															Baggage and Express Trains	
TRAIN NUMBERS →	211	213	215	217	219	221	223	225	227	229	231	233	235	237	239	511	
STATIONS	AM	AM	AM	AM	AM	AM	PM	PM	PM	PM	PM	PM	PM	PM	PM	PM	AM
Lv. Dallas	......	5 30	7 30	8 30	9 30	11 30	1 30	2 30	3 30	4 30	5 30	6 30	7 30	9 30	11 10	11 50	§11 30
" Oak Cliff Junction	......	5 40	7 40	8 40	9 40	11 40	1 40	2 40	3 40	4 40	5 40	6 40	7 40	9 40	11 20	12 00	§11 40
" Monroe	......	5 49	7 49	8 49	9 49	11 49	1 49	2 49	3 49	4 49	5 49	6 49	7 49	9 49	11 29	12 05	§11 49
" Lisbon	......	5 54	7 54	8 54	9 54	11 54	1 54	2 54	3 54	4 54	5 54	6 54	7 54	9 54	11 35	12 07	§11 54
" Lancaster	......	6 07	8 07	9 07	10 07	12 07	2 07	3 07	4 07	5 07	6 07	7 07	8 07	10 07	11 48	12 23	§12 07
" Red Oak	......	6 17	8 17	9 17	10 17	12 17	2 17	3 17	4 17	5 17	6 17	7 17	8 17	10 17	11 58	12 35	§12 17
" Sterrett	......	6 22	8 22	9 22	10 22	12 22	2 22	3 22	4 22	5 22	6 22	7 22	8 22	10 22	12 03	12 40	§12 22
" Waxahachie	......	6 34	8 34	9 34	10 34	12 34	2 34	3 34	4 34	5 34	6 34	7 34	8 34	10 34	12 15	1 00	§12 34
" Forreston	......	6 48	8 48	9 48	10 48	12 48	2 48	3 48	4 48	5 48	6 48	7 48	8 48	10 48	......	1 17	§12 48
" Italy	......	6 56	8 56	9 56	10 56	12 56	2 56	3 56	4 56	5 56	6 56	7 56	8 56	10 56	......	1 40	§12 56
" Milford	......	7 06	9 06	10 06	11 06	1 06	3 06	4 06	5 06	6 06	7 06	8 06	9 06	11 06	......	1 55	§1 06
" Hillsboro	‡6 40	7 28	9 28	10 28	11 28	1 28	3 28	4 28	5 28	6 28	7 28	8 28	9 28	11 28	......	2 33	§1 28
" Abbott	‡6 56	7 44	9 44	10 44	11 44	1 44	3 44	4 44	5 44	6 44	7 44	8 44	9 44	11 44	......	2 55	§1 44
" West	‡7 06	7 53	9 53	10 53	11 53	1 53	3 53	4 53	5 53	6 53	7 53	8 53	9 53	11 53	......	3 10	§1 53
" Elm Mott	‡7 21	8 05	10 05	11 05	12 05	2 05	4 05	5 05	6 05	7 05	8 05	9 05	10 05	12 05	......	3 25	§2 05
Ar. Waco	‡7 40	8 25	10 25	11 25	12 25	2 25	4 25	5 25	6 25	7 25	8 25	9 25	10 25	12 25	......	3 45	§2 25
STATIONS	AM	AM	AM	AM	PM	PM	PM	PM	PM	PM	PM	PM	PM	AM	AM	AM	PM

NORTHBOUND—WACO TO DALLAS (Read Down)

	PASSENGER TRAINS															Baggage and Express Trains	
TRAIN NUMBERS →	210	212	214	216	218	220	222	224	226	228	230	232	234	236	238	512	514
STATIONS	AM	AM	AM	AM	AM	AM	AM	PM	PM	PM	PM	PM	PM	PM	PM	PM	PM
Lv. Waco	......	......	5 10	7 00	8 00	9 00	11 00	1 00	2 00	3 00	4 00	5 00	6 00	7 00	9 00	‡12 10	6 30
" Elm Mott	......	......	5 30	7 21	8 21	9 21	11 21	1 21	2 21	3 21	4 21	5 21	6 21	7 21	9 21	‡12 30	6 50
" West	......	......	5 42	7 34	8 34	9 34	11 34	1 34	2 34	3 34	4 34	5 34	6 34	7 34	9 34	‡12 50	7 14
" Abbott	......	......	5 52	7 44	8 44	9 44	11 44	1 44	2 44	3 44	4 44	5 44	6 44	7 44	9 44	‡1 00	7 27
" Hillsboro	......	......	6 05	7 58	8 58	9 58	11 58	1 58	2 58	3 58	4 58	5 58	6 58	7 58	9 58	‡1 14	8 03
" Milford	......	......	6 25	8 17	9 17	10 17	12 17	2 17	3 17	4 17	5 17	6 17	7 17	8 17	10 17	‡1 45	8 30
" Italy	......	......	6 37	8 27	9 27	10 27	12 27	2 27	3 27	4 27	5 27	6 27	7 27	8 27	10 27	‡2 20	8 56
" Forreston	......	......	6 48	8 35	9 35	10 35	12 35	2 35	3 35	4 35	5 35	6 35	7 35	8 35	10 35	‡2 36	9 05
" Waxahachie	......	6 35	7 01	8 51	9 51	10 51	12 51	2 51	3 51	4 51	5 51	6 51	7 51	8 51	10 51	‡3 08	9 35
" Sterrett	......	6 45	7 12	9 01	10 01	11 01	1 01	3 01	4 01	5 01	6 01	7 01	8 01	9 01	11 01	‡3 23	9 48
" Red Oak	......	6 50	7 17	9 06	10 06	11 06	1 06	3 06	4 06	5 06	6 06	7 06	8 06	9 06	11 06	‡3 32	9 55
" Lancaster	‡6 18	7 02	7 27	9 18	10 18	11 18	1 18	3 18	4 18	5 18	6 18	7 18	8 18	9 18	11 18	‡3 45	10 17
" Lisbon	‡6 30	7 14	7 38	9 30	10 30	11 30	1 30	3 30	4 30	5 30	6 30	7 30	8 30	9 30	11 30	‡4 05	10 29
" Monroe	‡6 35	7 21	7 43	9 35	10 35	11 35	1 35	3 35	4 35	5 35	6 35	7 35	8 35	9 35	11 35	‡4 11	10 33
" Oak Cliff Junction	‡6 42	7 27	7 52	9 42	10 42	11 42	1 42	3 42	4 42	5 42	6 42	7 42	8 42	9 42	11 42	‡4 20	10 42
Ar. Dallas	‡6 55	7 40	8 05	9 55	10 55	11 55	1 55	3 55	4 55	5 55	6 55	7 55	8 55	9 55	11 55	‡4 30	10 52
STATIONS	AM	AM	AM	AM	AM	AM	PM	PM	PM	PM	PM	PM	PM	PM	PM	PM	PM

‡-Does not run on Sundays.
§-Express trailer operated on regular 11:30 A. M. Passenger Car daily, except Sunday
All trains on this division carry Baggage and Preferred Express.

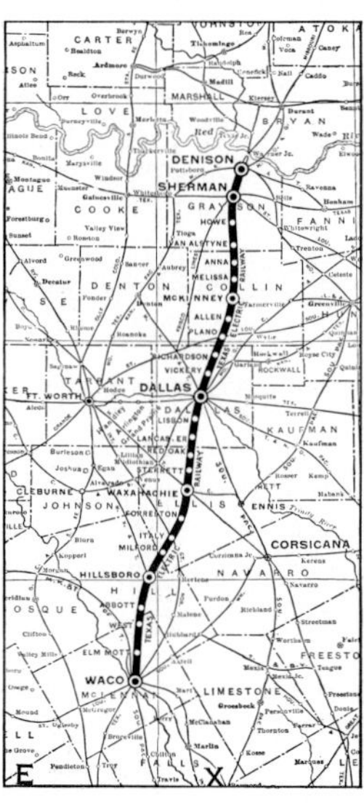

WINTER WONDERLAND. One of the rare times during a winter that Dallas has any snowfall gave the photographer a chance to show the big red and cream interurbans in a setting of pure white. This snow is the wet, sticky type which clings to everything. Even the line poles, crossarms and insulators have a coating of fluff. Here is the morning mail train, No. 10, and doing the honors is snow-topped car 362. We're just south of Matilda outbound from Dallas. By noon, all that wonderful whiteness will have melted away. Photo from M.D. McCarter.

SMOKY ATMOSPHERE is normal for this part of the Trinity River trestle at the point where it leaps the tracks of the Dallas Union Terminal. Usually, D.U.T. 0-6-0 engine No. 7 is puffing somewhere nearby rearranging passenger coaches. This time it looks like one of Dallas' industries is adding to the somberness of the day. Car No. 328 wearing flags and bound for Waco is passing car 315 headed for the Dallas Interurban Terminal. (MC)

SECOND ONLY TO DALLAS, Waco was a busy stretch of trackage for the Texas Electric. This early 'forties East Waco scene shows the crossover track that allows the northbound traffic to take to the single-track main on the right. Track on the lower left is that of the local city car line to the Bellmead M-K-T railroad shops. East Waco phone booth is due to be moved back closer to the East Waco spur, at the end of the visible track in this picture. Don't worry, that's a spring switch in the foreground! (TERA)

DALLAS
FRONT ENTRANCE
360
360

TEXAS ELECTRIC RAILWAY
371

THE INSIDE STORY. Here's an interior view of a Texas Electric coach, evidently made while the car was in motion. Shot from the motorman's cab, it shows the smoking or forward section with its beveled glass and highly polished oak partition. Signal cord still in place serves as a reminder of when both platforms had an attendant. (TERA)

Top, opposite.

HERE ON THE SHOP TRACKS at McKinney, RPO car 360's exterior shows it is in between modernization programs. Starting out as coach No. 11, it was remodeled to mail service when RPO No. 351 was rebuilt back to coach status. Railway mail service was instituted August 15, 1914, between Dallas and Denison. It continued until December 31, 1948, when the Texas Electric Railway came to the end of its existence. (TERA)

Bottom, opposite.

A MAGNIFICENT REMINDER of the Northern Texas Traction Co., "The Route of the Crimson Limiteds" to Fort Worth. No. 371 was inherited by TE when the NTT line closed down in 1934. Motor 371, shown here in the Dallas Interurban Terminal, started life as NTT 32 and held on to its leaded glass arch windows to the very end. Center section inside the coach shows the luxury of parlor chairs. A classic car—with sides of wood as an interurban should! Photo from Charles A. Smallwood.

Bridging the Brazos

TEXAS ELECTRIC CROSSED some major rivers, not to mention hundreds of assorted creeks, washes, draws, gullies and not a few railroads and highways. This is the Brazos River bridge at Waco, one of the major TE structures. The piers show successive rings of high water marks. In fact, the river was known to reach the ties during peak periods of rain in the hills above the city. Upstream is to your right as evidenced by the brush piled against the forward pier. After TE shut down operations the bridge deck was paved over and continued in use as a highway span, affording some relief to the Roebling swinging span just to the left of this scene. In 1975 the interurban bridge was being dismantled as completion of the new Interstate 35 east of this point has finally rendered the bridge obsolete after slightly more than 52 years of service. Photo from M.D. McCarter.

THIS VIEW of the interurban bridge over the Brazos looks downstream. The 1870 wire rope Roebling bridge, with its 473-foot swing over the stream was the longest single span in the world at the time of its construction. Visible behind the TE bridge, it is no longer in use but will remain as a museum piece. (I)

THIS IS WHAT THE MOTORMAN SAW crossing the Brazos River bridge. Waco is ahead, and the wire rope Roebling bridge is on the left (above). Bottom photo is a motorman's view of the track entering the 200-foot-long, three-truss Brazos interurban bridge from the south side of the river, opposite the Waco business district. Believe it or not, that's a block signal three quarters of the way up the pole projecting up in front of the left-hand tower of the Roebling highway bridge. Billboards seem to be positioned more for the benefit of interurban passengers than for motorists. (Both, TERA)

A TEXAS TRACTION TRIO: This is a three-car meet on the "East Line" at the south end of the Trinity Heights trestle. This location, known as Compton, caused occasional lineups like this as the double track merged into single track to cross the valley containing a small stream and the Santa Fe Railway. Car 308 is just coming off the single iron, southbound, while No. 307 waits patiently. The Trinity Heights local car of Stone & Webster ancestry would like to get going, too. Local car is in Dallas Railways livery, so this is a mid-1940s photo. Block signal governing the forward movement of the two standing cars is on a pole and is just visible above the right rear of No. 308. Building in the distance behind the 308 is the Hormel packing plant which was the last customer of Texas Electric Railway. Even though all other service stopped on December 31, 1948, the plant had to be served by TE until the Santa Fe could put in its own connection more than six months later. Photo from M.D. McCarter.

Toting the tonnage...

LIKE MANY INTERURBANS, Texas Electric got into the freight game late but it jumped in with both feet. A good volume of interchange tonnage was carried, and freight trains and box motor movements were much in evidence all over the system. This river bottom view shows a Class A motor leading two freight cars and an idling Class B (or C) loco across the Trinity River viaduct towards Oak Cliff. The difference between the classes of motors is easily spotted by observing the three side windows characteristic of Class A hogs. In zero weather the Charles City Western Railway, in Iowa, new owners of former TE motor 801, insist there are too many windows. But a summer day in Texas is something else. Photo from M.D. McCarter.

AS SOON AS PERMISSION to start freight operations was granted in the late 1920s, Monroe Shops took on new life. Walter Silvus, superintendent of motive power and general manager, began work building freight locomotives. Using 27MCB 3X trucks, with 5x9-in. journals, K-64-D controllers, four GE73C motors, 14E1 Westinghouse airbrakes, 2 CP28 air compressors and Ohio Brass form 23 couplers, they managed to fabricate a compact and efficient electric prime mover. Three of these Class A motors were built in 1929-30 complete with poling poles and sockets. They were numbered 801-803. Photo by Robert P. Townley.

EXPRESS MOTOR is halted in downtown Dallas giving Bob Townley a good chance to snap No. 503 on a clear and no doubt hot day in August, 1948. If you don't believe it is hot, note that everything that can be opened is open.

EXPRESS TRAIN No. 514 is stopped at East Waco while the motorman steps down to phone the dispatcher. It is shortly after his 6:30PM departure from the Waco terminal, and he has until 10:52PM to make it to Big D. The consist also includes trail car 603 not much altered from its original builders plans, but that end trailer is one of those three ex-Dallas Southern Traction Co. parlor cars successively numbered 455, 456 and 457, then A, B and C and finally 618, 619 and 620 as express trail cars. Photo from M.D. McCarter.

WITH OAK CLIFF STREETCARS on close headways, and frequent interurban trains as well to contend with, tieups in downtown Dallas were inevitable when it came time to jockey freight motors around. Jefferson Street (now Record) got busy when the freight and express depot hostlers decided to move a motor from one track to another. They are holding up a Dallas Railway ex-Peter Witt 700-series car and what looks like Train No. 224 due at the Dallas Interurban Terminal at 3:55PM. But, TE No. 305 is carrying a flag so it just could be a special movement. Both of these passenger cars have just come off the Trinity River viaduct which spans the Dallas Union Terminal railroad tracks as well. Photo from M.D. McCarter.

A HEAP O' FREIGHT MOTORS: While Texas Electric had 18 of these express motors, it was seldom that a photographer could catch as many as four in one place. Here on the Dallas freight terminal storage tracks is a mixed bag of express motors lined up for their picture—all saying "cheese." No. 509 sports a white marker flag, No. 508 shows off its arch windows; our favorite lens subject No. 502 hangs back a bit in false modesty while No. 503 wears a slatted cap. A great bunch of high-steppers. Photo from M.D. McCarter.

TWO CLASS A FREIGHT MOTORS. Top, No. 801 rests on the Waco carbarn shop track. All motors working south of Monroe Shops had to have 1,200-volt capability as well as 600v. The higher voltage was inherited from the parent Southern Traction and never changed. No. 801 survives to this day as Iowa Terminal No. 53 after an interim stint as Charles City Western 303. Bottom photo is of Class A motor 802 at Monroe Shops. Details show up loud and clear: sand tanks, two headlights, an auxiliary motor generator, train run number box and lots of lights under the eaves (these motors looked like Christmas trees at night!). Metal boxes on the platforms were used for storing gear. (Both, TERA)

JUST ACROSS THE BRAZOS RIVER, the Waco city cars and the interurbans shared a long double track on a curve. It really was a passing track capable of holding the traffic which had to line up to enter the single track on the bridge as well as the single track on Elm Street which extended for three blocks behind the photographer. Express motor 506 is Train No. 511 leaving Waco Terminal at 12:15PM. It will take four hours to reach Dallas. Local car 252 inbound from East Waco will make a slight dogleg to the left and thread its way through the bridge girders in far background. Finally it will deliver its full load of passengers downtown. Photo from M.D. McCarter.

A PROUD DAY FOR THE TEXAS ELECTRIC: The first day of freight interchange with a steam railroad, May 1, 1928. Officials of the juice line had been working toward this event since 1924. T&NO (Texas & New Orleans) car No. 34783 originated at Waco and is now at Italy and will soon be spotted on the Missouri Pacific lines interchange track. Route from there will be to Fort Worth where it will be handed over to the Texas Pacific to be hauled to its ultimate destination at Odessa. Almost as many officials are gathered for this event as were on hand for the opening day of passenger service. Waco veteran photographer "Gildy" Gildersleeve was on hand to record the event; motive power for this festive occasion was line car 901. C.V. Hess Collection.

LUCKY THEY HAD SOME WIDE STREETS in Waco, what with the maneuvering that Texas Electric combo has to do. Express motor 506 leads trail car in a demonstration of how radial couplers are supposed to work. The lead car is first No. 506, ex 357, ex-ex No. 8 and will get another rebuilding to finish life as No. 511. The car being hauled started out on the north end of the system as No. 53, a combine designed for newspaper and passenger service. Converted to a pure express motor it became No. 553 and continued that way until one day it was downgraded to trail status, losing its 27MCB trucks in favor of arch-bar freight trucks and renumbered 602. Photo from M.D. McCarter.

THIS CAN'T BE ANYTHING ELSE but Train No. 221 (above) somewhere in Central Texas. Passenger motor 319 is hauling one of the ex-parlor cars on its 2-hour, 55-minute, 97-mile run between Dallas and Waco. It left Big D at 11:30AM and is due in Waco at 2:25PM. This train ran seven days a week, except for the trailer—never on Sunday. Bottom photo is another shot of our friend, express motor 502 (we have lots of photos of this beauty). One of the trail cars can prove it was once a more important part of the railroad as it proudly wears its two trolley bases, sans poles. We'd guess this scene to be between Hobson and Glendale, probably near Lisbon siding. Both photos from M.D. McCarter.

DYNAMIC DUO: Class B locomotives also had 1,200-volt capability and were numbered 902-906. They were definitely built from ex-passenger motors; shown above is 903, ex No. 361, ex-ex No. 12. Motor 902 was created from first No. 314, No. 904 from No. 325 while No. 905 was formed by rebuilding car 304. We notice that there is no provision on Class B locomotives (or Class C for that matter) for poling movements. Bottom photo is of motor 906, converted from first 317 (second No. 311) and like its sister it could handle about eight loaded freight cars very well. It's shown here at Monroe Shops. Cage-like apparatus inside the cab (look sharp and maybe you can see it) encloses the group switches which responded to the motorman's manipulation of the controller. (Both, TERA)

THIS CLASS C MOTOR is on the Sherman yard tracks and is hiding the Sherman-Denison tripper car which is halted on another track. Nice neat row of resistance grids is visible under the freight motor. This motor is presumably ex-No. 356, ex-ex No. 7 but the former numbers are in doubt. There were three locomotives in this group; No. 952 (ex-353, ex-ex No. 4) is alive and well and living in San Antonio as Texas Transportation Co. No. 2. Nowadays it hauls some of the makings of Pearl beer. Photo from M.D. McCarter.

HERE's a Class C locomotive parked on an interchange track at Denison. No. 951 (one of three 600v motors rebuilt from passenger cars) is ex-352, ex-ex-3. Photo by Robert P. Townley.

TALK ABOUT A GRAVEYARD RUN! It is the East Waco spur which served as a freight interchange with the Cotton Belt (St. Louis & Southwestern RR). It was something like four blocks long and left the main line at Elm Street where the East Waco local car line terminated. No. 503 is on the passing track headed for the freight station. The motorman is using the "B" end of the motor, in effect running backward so they can run forward with whatever load they pick up. Front end of these cars didn't usually have a train door. Not too well-kept-up cemetery is at right. Photo from M.D. McCarter.

DOZING IN THE TEXAS SUN: This former passenger coach, express motor 510, awaits its next summons to duty. Long ago it was No. 5 of the first series of Texas Traction Co. cars; later it became No. 354 and was remodeled again to become second No. 359. Now, as an express motor it sees occasional service as a Dallas-to-Denison baggage-express. (TERA)

STRICTLY UTILITARIAN: Showing evidence on the dash and windows of having been towed during a rainstorm, express motor 502 stands parked at Monroe Shops. This is one of the 500-505 class that Southern Traction Co. ordered for the start of operations in 1913. Now the gold striping and big headlights are gone and the letterboards and baggage doors seem to have disappeared in favor of a no-nonsense boxcar look. Not that these motors didn't have a certain charm right to the end, though. Photo from M.D. McCarter.

YOU COULDN'T CALL IT A GLAMOR PUSS, but motor 501 went about its business efficiently. Here, as baggage-express southbound train No. 12, it is on the Italy house track with loading dock on the left and warehouse on the right. The main track is almost half a block to the right of this warehouse. Turnout in the left foreground is the beginning of an interchange track leading to the Missouri Pacific Railway lines. Photo from M.D. McCarter.

STILL AT WORK in the Lone Star State is Texas Transportation Co. motor 2. It now serves the Pearl Brewery in San Antonio hauling inbound cars of grain and tank cars of corn syrup from the Southern Pacific interchange, and, of course, outbound shipments of beer. Until 1949 it was Texas Electric 952, built by Brill in 1908 as interurban passenger car No. 4 of the Texas Traction. Photo by Joe R. Thompson.

NICE VIEW of the Hillsboro passenger and freight station. One express trailer occupies the house track just now. A transformer station also was located on this property, out of the picture to the left. Photo from M.D. McCarter.

TOO BAD SOME TROLLEY MUSEUM didn't latch on to this one. Yard motor No. X2 has seen better days, all right. In fact, oldtimers say it was even used to tow line materials on the Waco streetcar lines. In this view it sits out of everybody's way in a corner of the Waco yard, boxed in by the city trolley and the Ford Transit bus. Wonder what No. X1 looked like? (TERA)

On city streets

ONE THING THAT DISTINGUISHED an interurban from a line haul railroad was street running, and Texas Electric had a lot of street running. In the cities as well as the towns. This is afternoon train No. 227 outbound in Dallas shortly after its 3:30PM departure time from the Interurban Terminal. Let's let Walter Donalson explain the sequence of movement: "Car 328 after having left the terminal on Wood Street, moved right on to Akard for two blocks and then left on Commerce, turned left again on to Jefferson Street (now Record) and proceeded two blocks where it is now crossing Wood Street (above). The turret of the Dallas County Courthouse is visible in the extreme left of the picture. Wye tracks in the photo form the exit from the TE Express Terminal which is to the right of the car." August 1948 photo by Robert P. Townley.

NORTH OF DALLAS IS McKINNEY, and that's where we are as we see motor 310 (ex-316) running as train 14 picking up some revenue on a hot August day in 1948. If this car is on time it is 2:24PM. That young lady is stretching her skirt to make that first step. Today's young lady—no problem at all. No interurban, either. Photo by Robert P. Townley.

AN IMPORTANT CITY CAR LINE was operated by Texas Electric in Dallas. It was the Trinity Heights line across the Trinity River viaduct into Oak Cliff and then south along the Waco main line to the southern Dallas city limits. The little Stone & Webster "turtleback" cars used on this line seated about 40 passengers and were fairly fast 'n frisky. Fare? Only a nickel. In the early years there also was a branch south on Zangs from Jefferson Blvd. which linked up with the main line at the Monroe Shops; if you made the complete circuit, the fare doubled to 10¢. Toward the end of operation, the local line was taken over by Dallas Railway & Terminal. P.C. McPherson Jr. notes that the TE also operated local service at various times in Waxahachie, McKinney, Denison, Sherman, Corsicana and Waco, the latter operation actually outliving the interurbans at least briefly. This fine glass negative is owned by Charles A. Smallwood.

THOSE WACO CITY CARS did get banged up a bit. This dented Stone & Webster type is at the East Waco end of the line. Motorman has already reversed the poles and seats. A passenger has just come aboard and the doors have been folded shut. With both hands on the controls our dauntless operator will use a crossover (out of sight to the left) to get on the inbound track and will soon scoot onto Elm Street. Destination: downtown Waco. (I)

Top, opposite.

ANOTHER TURTLEBACK, this time in Waco, is a rare Bellmead loading scene. The dash shows the dirt and mud splashes caused by p/rw running which occurs after the tracks leave the pavement beyond East Waco. Front trolley rope is wound around the headlight; trolley catcher probably has a weak spring. In fact, the whole car looks to be a bit weary. (TERA)

Bottom, opposite.

THIS CLOSE-UP OF A MAXIMUM-TRACTION truck under a Waco city car gives you a chance to study the springing and other detail. The framework above the pony wheel was called a "knee" by shopmen and served to support the loading platform. (Some operators said these trucks were misnamed as minimum traction might be more like it.) (TERA)

A MEET ON THE STREET; Passenger motor 350 is carrying the mail on Bryan Street in Dallas; express motor 509 hauling a trailer is running extra, or so that white flag flapping on the front end tells us. The big green express car is crossing Haskell Avenue as the colorful red, cream and silver-roofed passenger coach rolls by the Southwestern Bell Telephone building, circa 1946. This corner was also a stop for the green-and-cream Belmont city line cars. Photo from M.D. McCarter.

DOWN A SHADY LANE rumbles a two-section Texas Electric train on its way to Denison. Because of the presence of unused track on the right, Walter Donalson Jr. believes that this scene is possibly Brockette Avenue, near Maxey Street, in Sherman. Photo by Robert W. Richardson.

OFF IN THE DISTANCE, Waxahachie Courthouse tower looms, placing No. 302 on North College Street headed for Dallas. Photo from M.D. McCarter.

TEXAS ELECTRIC TOOK ITS OBLIGATIONS seriously—especially the need to keep the property in repair. Express motor 502 doubles in this view as a work train motor in Hillsboro. Track workers are patching the street just south of the downtown area. Photo from M.D. McCarter.

JUST TAKES YOUR BREATH AWAY, this arch-windowed beauty. Every rivet shows in this Charles D. Savage photo. Here you have a chance to see how trolley pole retrievers (catchers?) were positioned and how the wheel pole always rode hooked down. The small loop on the left front underbody is the handle for pulling the pin on the coupler, and the rear pin puller handle is visible under the right rear. Car 315 is leaving the terminal area in downtown Corsicana on April 9, 1940. The next time this car enters Monroe Shops for rebuilding it will lose the arch windows (ah, progress!) and emerge as second 316.

INBOUND IN DOWNTOWN WACO it is hard to tell if this is Train No. 213 or 223. Judging by the angle of the sunlight it is late afternoon so it is probably 223 arriving in Waco at 4:25PM. Which leads P.C. McPherson Jr. to comment of this mini-series of cars (325-328): "These cars were purchased about 1926. They had three notches on the controller and automatically fed six more as speed picked up. They had storage batteries in case the trolley jumped or a breaker went out—in their day they were a great attraction in the electric transportation field. Originally all cars were olive green, but in later years to keep up with the times various stripes and colors were added." (TERA)

BOUNCING BIRNEYS AND THEIR BIG BROTHERS: In better days, local rail transportation was to be found on the streets of Dallas and Waco, and in both cities this sometimes meant the little Birney Safety Car was on the loose. Top view shows Austin Street in Waco, looking north. Drat that flivver for obscuring our view of the Texas Electric Birney, but this mid-1920s shot shows that motorists had to try hard to find a parking space then, too. Today there is no parking here at all as the "Save the Downtown" effort has converted the whole street to a mall. The bottom view is of Commerce Street in downtown Dallas, mid-1940s, at the corner of Poydras. Waco bound car 309 has flags indicating it is the first section of this run and is being followed closely by the second section just beyond the Dallas Railway Birney. The city car at left is one of the 700 series ex-Peter Witts which were the strength of the Dallas streetcar system. Like Waco, there have been some changes made. Not only are the trolleys and their tracks missing, but all the buildings in the foreground have disappeared as well, including the hotel. It is progress. Isn't it? (Top, TERA; Bottom, I)

And in the end...

WHEN TEXAS ELECTRIC THREW IN THE TOWEL on the last day of 1948, it was truly the end of an era. The proud TE stuck it out longer than most, but late in the year the line's directors made the decision they viewed as inevitable: get out while the getting was good. Traffic was plummeting as new postwar automobiles flooded the roads, but there was still a little money left to tidy things up at the end and to bow out with grace and style. December 31, 1948, was a day for picture-taking, goodbyes and reminiscing as the cars rolled their last. For many of the line's faithful employes, retirement would commence on the morrow, the first day of 1949. At left, on the afternoon of the last day, one such operator whose name we unfortunately do not have prepares to board at Waxahachie the last car to Dallas. Photo by Margaret Ramage.

LAST INTERURBAN TO WACO: Below is the crowd at Waxahachie greeting the end of the Texas Electric era—in this case the last car from Dallas. The southbound red and cream car is loading at the usual position opposite the Interurban Station in a store building at right. The crowd seems more interested in getting its picture taken than in the arrival of car 328, but that's human nature. This view looks north on College Street, late afternoon, December 31, 1948. Tomorrow Waxahachie will be just like all the other interurban-less towns. Photo by Margaret Ramage.

THE LAST STRAW: The dejected stance of the man in the foreground seems to say the end is near. The track and wrecker crew are attempting to re-rail the two cars that came together in the spectacular headon collision north of Vickery on April 10, 1948. Some say this was the tragedy that did Texas Electric in. Forty-nine persons were injured, and while a very serious thing, this was only one of the factors leading to the end of service. An ICC investigation of the accident blamed issuance of a lap order by the TE dispatcher which put two opposing trains heading toward each other on single track. Cars 366 and 365 hit headon on a blind curve. (TERA)

Big D was Big Time in traction

OH, MY, TEXAS DID HAVE CLASS when it came to interurbans. Let us close our study of traction out of Big D by sampling two other operations. This is a posed view of the Crimson Limited, the Northern Texas Traction Company's flagship. The location is at the barn on East Lancaster Street in Fort Worth just beyond the private right of way. You might have thought that the strategic Dallas-Fort Worth interurban link would outlast everything else, but the NTT was gone by 1934, a good decade and a half prior to the demise of the Texas Electric. Photo from Charles A. Smallwood.

ULTRAMODERN FOR THE 1920s was the Texas Interurban Company's Dallas-Terrell line. The TI wasn't built until 1923 making it just about the last new interurban constructed in the U.S. save for the Texas North Shore out of Houston which was built four years later. The Terrell route was quite a contrast to the company's other route, to Denton which was on electrified leased M-K-T line tracks. This lightweight car was one of eleven (100-110) and had an upright whistle above the right front window and what must have been the tallest trolley tower and hold down hook in the nation. In this scene the car is already well past the town of Mesquite and on its way into Big D, which it will enter over the Dallas Railway's Forney line. Walter Donalson's best guess is that this photo was taken on what might possibly be today's Military Parkway. The TI, which was built as an appendage of the Dallas city system in an effort to get a franchise extended, expired in less than 10 years. Photo from Charles A. Smallwood.

FADING INTO THE DISTANCE, there goes the Crimson Limited of the Northern Texas Traction Co. on its way to Fort Worth. Soon it will disappear over the horizon, and we shall not see it again just as we will not see the red and cream beauties of the Texas Electric rails save through the camera's lens and the memories of those who lived the interurban era in the Lone Star State. Photo from Charles A. Smallwood.